COOKIES GALORE

COOKIES GALORE

JACQUELINE BELLEFONTAINE

Published by MQ Publications Limited
12 The Ivories, 6–8 Northampton Street
London N1 2HY
Tel: 44 (0)20 7359 2244
Fax: 44 (0)20 7359 1616
email: mail@mqpublications.com
website: www.mqpublications.com

North American office
49 West 24th Street
New York, NY 10010
Email: information@mqpublicationsus.com

Website: www.mqpublications.com

PHOTOGRAPHY: Marie Louise Avery & Chris Alack (see page 192)
DESIGN CONCEPT & LAYOUT: Clare Barber
RECIPE CREDITS: see page 192

ISBN (13): 978-1-84601-199-3
ISBN (10): 1-84601-199-X

1 3 5 7 9 0 8 6 4 2

Printed and bound in China

CONTENTS

INTRODUCTION

Nothing can beat the aroma of a freshly baked cookie. Home-made cookies make a wonderful gift to brighten someone's day and they are great fun to make with children.

★ ORIGINS ★

The word cookie has become commonplace all over the world but in Britain the word biscuit is also used. Cookie comes from the Dutch word *koekje* and means little cake. Biscuit on the other hand comes from the French *bis cuit* and means twice cooked. This harks back to the days when bakers put slices of fresh baked bread back in the oven to dry out and they became hard like rusks. This of course improved the keeping qualities, and was especially important when such foods were taken on long sea voyages and had to keep for a long length of time. Nowadays, soft cake-like confections are known as cookies (choc chip cookies for example) whereas crisper versions, such as shortbread are known as biscuits.

Apart from the obvious satisfaction which comes from making your own cookies, there is the added advantage that you can use the best ingredients and know exactly what they contain. Cookies are easy to make and many in this book are of the free-form kind, which you either spoon on to a tray or shape with your hands, so no extra equipment is needed. Home-made cookies are always popular so if you refrain from making them because they will all disappear in a flash, then make the refrigerator type where you slice off the raw dough as you need them or make sure you have some freezer bags handy to pop some in the deep freeze. Cookies are not only great as a mid-morning treat, they are also good in lunchboxes and make a great quick dessert when accompanied by ice cream or thick fruity yogurt.

★ GET BAKING ★

There is something very therapeutic about baking cookies – it is to do with allowing ourselves to play again. Children love baking and you can have such fun with them, so don't just look at the wonderful pictures in this book – get baking and bring pleasure to yourself and those you love.

EQUIPMENT

To bake good cookies you don't need fancy equipment but here are a few tips on items you will need.

★ BOWLS ★

These can be of glass, ceramic or stainless steel, it does not matter which, but what is important if you are using a hand-held electric mixer is that the bowl is tall and deep rather than wide and shallow. Sugar, flour and especially icing sugar tend to fly out of a shallow bowl.

★ HAND-HELD ELECTRIC MIXER ★

Although not absolutely necessary, a hand-held electric mixer is so handy and quick for creaming butter and sugar and for beating egg whites.

★ MEASURES ★

A set of measuring cups and spoons is vital for measuring quantities down to a fraction of a teaspoon. The amounts given in the recipes are for level cupfuls and spoonfuls unless stated otherwise. A set of scales is also desirable as cookies, like cakes, require accurate measuring of ingredients.

★ TIMER ★

Timing is vital – cookies are easily overcooked if left a few minutes too long, so a timer with a loud ring will keep you alerted.

★ BAKING SHEETS & BROWNIE TINS ★

Cookies can burn easily so it is wise to buy heavy professional quality sheets and tins. Every tin will bake a little differently depending on the weight, thickness and material it's made from. Lining with baking paper helps promote even baking as does placing a thin baking sheet or brownie tin on top of another baking sheet for extra insulation. Baking sheets should be rimless or with low rims so that it is easy to remove the cookies. Air-cushioned baking sheets bake evenly but they may take a little longer and generally are better when you want to end up with soft chewy cookies rather than crisp ones.

★ SIFTER ★

A sifter is good to have although not essential. It's often used for sifting icing sugar over the cookies, and if you have a tea strainer that will do the job just as well.

★ PASTRY BRUSH ★

A brush is very handy for brushing away surplus flour, greasing tins and brushing on egg or glazes. Buy a good quality brush that has firmly fixed bristles.

★ ROLLING PIN ★

Cookie dough is often rolled out to quite a large size so it is preferable to have a rolling pin that is straight and without handles. Other than that choose one that is comfortable for you.

★ CUTTERS ★

Some recipes require cutters. There are many cutters available in myriad shapes and sizes. For best results the cutter should be sharp and have a good clear outline. This generally means that they should be made of metal rather than plastic, but some plastic versions do have a sharp enough edge. To use a cutter, place gently on the dough and then using the palm of your hand press firmly and evenly down on the cutter. Lift the cutter off without twisting it. Some doughs may be slightly sticky or moist so it is a good idea to dip the edge of the cutter in some flour every now and then.

★ KNIVES ★

A large sharp knife is good for cutting cleanly through rolled out or refrigerated dough. Even more useful are a couple of round-bladed spatulas, one large, one small. They are invaluable for spreading and smoothing mixtures, transferring cut out cookies to baking sheets and removing them once cooked. They can also be used for spreading icing or chocolate on to baked cookies.

★ BAKING PAPER ★

A roll of baking paper is good to have as it can be used to line baking sheets so cookies don't stick. It's also useful to sandwich soft or sticky dough when rolling out.

★ WIRE RACKS ★

These can be cheap and cheerful, it doesn't really matter. You can even use the rack from the grill pan, but a wire rack is necessary if you want crisp cookies as they will go soft if left on the baking sheet.

★ PIPING BAGS & NOZZLES ★

Again, these are not essential as only a few recipes in the book require them but if you do a lot of baking they are useful to have. You can buy disposable piping bags and plastic nozzles from most speciality kitchen shops.

★ AIRTIGHT STORAGE CONTAINERS ★

Home-made cookies can quickly lose their crispness in humid conditions so a few storage containers are vital.

INGREDIENTS

The finest ingredients make the finest cookies. Don't consider using up your shrivelled dried fruit and musty old spices in a batch of cookies. Choose your ingredients carefully and you will have cookies to die for.

BUTTER

Most of the recipes are best made with unsalted butter. Out of all the ingredients (other then chocolate) butter has the most effect on the flavour and texture of cookies so use the best that you can afford. Avoid using tub margarines, butter substitutes and spreads as these often contain a high percentage of water and will upset the balance of the recipe.

EGGS

Most of the recipes in this book use medium eggs unless stated otherwise. Farm fresh, organic or free-range eggs taste better and give a better result than battery eggs. Always use eggs at room temperature.

FLOUR

Flour does vary so always use a good premium brand and make sure it hasn't been hanging around too long. These days it is rare to find lumpy flour so sifting isn't always necessary but it does add more air, so making it easier to mix in. Don't sift wholemeal flour as you will be taking out all the goodness.

BAKING POWDER & BICARBONATE OF SODA

Some cookie recipes need extra help to rise and so need baking powder or bicarbonate of soda or sometimes both. Make sure they are fresh as they go stale quite quickly once opened. If you have some that has been hanging around for a while it is best to throw it out and treat yourself to a new pack to avoid disappointing results.

SUGAR

Generally speaking unrefined pure cane sugars have a deeper flavour and are preferable to use but this is not as important as the type of sugar specified in the recipe. The sugar is usually chosen for a particular

reason. For example, castor sugar has very small crystals which dissolve quickly and easily so it is ideal to use when creaming with fat. You can substitute the sugars in recipes but the results may not be as good.

CHOCOLATE

For the very best flavour always use plain chocolate with at least 70% cocoa solids. Unless stated in the recipe never use chocolate chips to replace chocolate which is to be melted or blended into the mixture as they are formulated to keep their shape when cooked and are sweeter and less smooth in texture. Some recipes call for milk or white chocolate so always look for the cooking variety and not confectionery bars.

LEMON & ORANGE RIND

Always use unwaxed fruit, which has been washed before use.

SPICES & EXTRACTS

All spices should be as fresh as possible. Only buy in small quantities and if they don't smell wonderfully fresh when opened then buy some more. Always use a quality, pure extract, it really makes a difference.

FRUIT & NUTS

Dried fruit should be moist and plump. Fruits such as dates are often better bought whole rather than pre-chopped. Nuts should be as fresh as possible as the oils they contain can turn rancid. Store opened packets in the freezer if you are not going to use them regularly. When chopping or grinding nuts in a food processor always use a perfectly dry bowl and use the pulse button, scraping them down occasionally. Using this method there is no danger of the nuts turning into a paste.

MAKING COOKIES with kids

Some of the first things young children learn to cook are little sweets, cakes and cookies.

★ REASONS WHY ★

The recipes are simple and don't involve lots of hot pans and sharp knives which are too dangerous for very young children. Not only is baking fun, it can also be a useful lesson in many subjects. Measuring, weighing and counting cookies is maths; washing hands, keeping things clean and tidy is hygiene; seeing what happens when air is beaten into egg whites is science; and decorating with sweets and icing is creative art! So an afternoon spent baking is not frivolous but huge fun and very educational.

Fussy eaters can often be encouraged to be more adventurous if they are allowed to help with cooking. A savoury cookie could be made for the child's lunch box – most children love eating the food they have made themselves.

Always allow plenty of time, especially when cooking with very young children, and remember they may often lose interest but then come back a few minutes later. It is worth being patient at this stage as a love of cooking and food instilled at a young age is very valuable.

★ SAFETY TIPS ★

Remember a kitchen can sometimes be dangerous for children so there are a few things worth considering.

★ Young children run everywhere so make sure they wear shoes with non-slip soles – trainers are ideal.

★ An apron or even a clean tea towel will protect their clothes from the food.

★ Make sure they wash their hands and tie back long hair. Keep a clean wet cloth handy for sticky fingers.

★ If they have to stand on a chair or stool to help, make sure it is secure – better if possible to let them mix and stir on a small table suitable to their height.

★ Place a wet cloth under mixing bowls and chopping boards as this will stop them from slipping.

★ Don't leave children alone with knives or electrical equipment.

★ A lot of the cookies in this book can be made much smaller – young children prefer tiny food. Just adjust the cooking time slightly.

★ Small children will find it easier to make drop cookies or those that they can roll into balls. Let older kids be creative with biscuits that are cut out and decorated.

★ The microwave is safer than the hob for young children to use when doing such things as melting chocolate.

★ Gather all the ingredients together before you start as children are eager to get going but can lose interest if they are waiting around.

★ Encourage a little judicious tasting (avoiding raw egg) to experience new flavours and textures – you don't have to wait until the cookies are cooked. Remember licking out the bowl as a child?

TROUBLESHOOTING

Use these essential questions and answers to dig yourself out of any cookie baking problems you come across.

Q – *The recipe calls for softened butter, what is this?*

A – If you are using an electric mixer the butter should be left at room temperature until it gives slightly when pressed. If you are using a wooden spoon the butter should be the consistency of thick mayonnaise. Butter can be softened in the microwave at 30% power.

Q – *The first tray of cookies I bake are always OK but the cookies on subsequent trays are often deformed – why is this?*

A – Always cool baking sheets before putting on a new batch of raw cookies. Warm sheets will start the dough melting slowly and this will cause the cookies to spread and become deformed.

Q – *I always find it difficult to measure very sticky ingredients such as golden syrup. How can I make it easier?*

A – To measure golden syrup and black treacle accurately open the can or jar and rest the lid on top. Place the can or jar in a bowl and fill with boiling water to halfway up the side of the can. Leave for a few minutes and then you will find the syrup is runny and easy to measure accurately.

Q – *I often find my dough to be very sticky and soft, so I add extra flour when rolling out, but then my biscuits turn out tough. What is the solution?*

A – Always refrigerate a dough rather than be tempted to add any extra flour. More flour equals a drier mixture, which will result in a tougher biscuit. Alternatively, roll out the dough between sheets of baking paper.

Q – *My cookies always seem to bake unevenly. Why is this?*

A – Always rotate the baking sheets halfway through the baking time. If you are baking more than one sheet of cookies at a time then reverse them top to bottom and front to back. Also make sure all the cookies are the same size. If you are unsure of your oven you can fine tune the baking of cookies by test baking 3 or 4 cookies first.

Q – *How can I make sure my drop cookies are all even-sized?*

A – A good trick is to use a small round ice cream scoop or lightly oiled measuring tablespoon.

Q – *I like to make cookies and usually make the drop variety—occasionally I would like to try other types but I don't have any cookie cutters.*

A – To cut cookie dough rounds without a cutter use a sturdy inverted wine glass. Or form small amounts of the dough into balls and flatten.

Q – *My cookies are often tough and dry, why is this?*

A – There could be a few reasons for this. Make sure your measuring is accurate. Do not overmix the dough once the flour has been added as this will cause the gluten to develop and create a tough cookie. The same applies to kneading and rolling out – keep it to a minimum and do not add extra flour. If the dough is sticky, chill it for a while and roll out between sheets of baking paper. It could also be that you are leaving the cookies in the oven too long. Even a minute or two extra can make them dry and tough, so remove them just before you think they are done as they will continue to cook for a short time.

AFTERNOON TEA

COCONUT Cookies

Rich cookies, with a strong coconut taste. Decorate them by dipping in chocolate or drizzling a little chocolate over the top.

MAKES: 24
BAKING TIME: 10–12 MINUTES

INGREDIENTS
125g butter
165g sugar
50ml coconut milk
75g flaked coconut
225g plain flour
2 teaspoons baking powder

ICING
25g icing sugar
2 tablespoons coconut milk
40g flaked coconut

1. Preheat the oven to 180°C/350°F/Gas mark 4. Lightly grease two baking sheets.

2. Cream the butter and sugar together until pale and fluffy. Beat in the coconut milk and flaked coconut.

3. Sift the flour and baking powder and work into the coconut mixture. Drop tablespoons of the dough well apart on the baking sheets. Bake until golden, 10–12 minutes. Cool on the baking sheets for 2–3 minutes, then transfer to a wire rack to cool completely.

4. To make the icing, sift the icing sugar into a bowl and stir in the coconut milk until smooth. Spread over the cookies, then sprinkle the coconut over the top. Dry until the icing sets, 1–2 hours. Store in an airtight container for up to five days.

BANANA & WALNUT Cookies

You could try using other types of nuts, but walnuts work particularly well with the smooth banana taste of these wholesome cookies.

MAKES: 20
BAKING TIME: 15 MINUTES

INGREDIENTS
225g plain flour
1 teaspoon baking powder
125g butter, cut into cubes
175g soft light brown sugar
100g walnuts, roughly chopped
2 small or 1 large banana, peeled
1 egg
50ml milk

1. Preheat the oven to 180°C/350°F/Gas mark 4. Lightly grease two baking sheets.

2. Sift the flour and baking powder into a bowl. Add the butter and blend with your fingertips until the mixture resembles fine breadcrumbs. Stir in the sugar and walnuts.

3. Mash the banana with a fork and beat in the egg. Stir in the milk. Add to the bowl and mix until well combined.

4. Drop spoonfuls of the dough on to the baking sheets, spacing well apart. Bake until golden, about 15 minutes. Transfer to a wire rack to cool completely. Store in a cool place for up to three days. Suitable for freezing for up to two months.

COOKIE TIP

To make cookie sandwiches, melt some chocolate chips. Using a spatula, spread the chocolate over two cookies and then press them together.

CITRUS CREAM Clouds

More like little cakes, these cookies would be good for special occasions such as a birthday tea.

MAKES: 18
BAKING TIME: 5–8 MINUTES

INGREDIENTS
180g butter
1 teaspoon finely grated lime rind
80g icing sugar
225g plain flour
40g cornflour

FILLING
125g unsalted butter at room temperature
1 teaspoon vanilla extract
1 teaspoon finely grated orange rind
1 teaspoon finely grated lemon rind
160g icing sugar, sifted
Icing sugar for dusting

1. Beat together the butter, lime rind, and icing sugar until smooth and creamy. Stir in the flour and cornflour and knead until smooth. Wrap in clingfilm and chill for 30 minutes until firm.

2. Roll out half the dough between sheets of baking paper. Using a flower-shaped cutter or a cutter of your choice cut out eighteen 4cm shapes.

3. Add any scraps of dough to the remaining pastry and roll out as before and cut out eighteen 6cm shapes.

4. Preheat the oven to 180°C/350°F/Gas mark 4. Place the shapes 2.5cm apart on baking sheets lined with baking paper. Bake in the oven for about 5–6 minutes for small shapes and 7–8 for large shapes, until lightly browned. Place on wire racks to cool.

5. Put all the filling ingredients into a bowl and beat together until smooth and creamy.

6. Either pipe or spread the filling on each of the larger cookies. Top each one with a smaller cookie. Dust with icing sugar to serve.

GINGER Crisps

These crisp ginger cookies look very impressive. You will need to work quickly, but once you get the hang of them, they are quite easy to make.

MAKES: 20
BAKING TIME: 5–6 MINUTES

INGREDIENTS
4 tablespoons butter
60g plain flour
1½ teaspoons ground ginger
½ teaspoon ground cinnamon
¼ teaspoon ground cloves
100g soft brown sugar
2 egg whites

1. Preheat the oven to 190°C/375°F/Gas mark 5. Lightly grease two baking sheets.

2. Melt the butter gently in a pan, then let it cool but not solidify.

3. Sift the flour and spices together, then sift again to ensure that they are well mixed and lightly aerated. Sift the brown sugar to remove any lumps.

4. Beat the egg whites until they stand in soft peaks. Gradually beat in the sugar. Carefully fold in the flour mixture. Drizzle in the butter and fold until just combined.

5. Place 2–3 heaped teaspoons of the dough on to a baking sheet and spread each one to form a 7.5cm round. Bake until just set and beginning to brown around the edges, 5–6 minutes. While one batch of cookies is cooking, spread the next one on the second baking sheet. Oil a rolling pin.

6. When baked, leave the cookies to stand for a few seconds. Then, working quickly before they set, carefully remove from the baking sheet with a slim spatula and place over the oiled rolling pin; they will cool in a curve. Remove from the rolling pin. Repeat until all the dough is baked. Store in an airtight container for two to three days.

LEMON MACADAMIA NUT Cookies

These cookies have a lovely lemon tang. They are fabulous served with creamy desserts.

MAKES: 24
BAKING TIME: 10–12 MINUTES

INGREDIENTS
125g butter, softened
100g sugar
2 egg yolks
Grated rind of ½ lemon
50ml lemon juice
225g plain flour
6 tablespoons cornflour
100g macadamia nuts, lightly chopped

1. Preheat the oven to 190°C/375°F/Gas mark 5. Lightly grease two baking sheets.

2. Cream the butter and sugar together until light and fluffy. Beat in the egg yolks, lemon rind, and juice.

3. Sift the flour and cornflour and beat into the mixture. Add the nuts and stir until well mixed.

4. Drop heaped tablespoons of the dough on to the baking sheets and flatten slightly with the back of a spoon.

5. Bake until golden, 10–12 minutes. Cool on the baking sheets for a few minutes before transferring to a wire rack to cool completely.

COOKIE TIP
If a recipe calls for both lemon rind and juice, pour the lemon juice over the rind to keep it moist.

MALTED DROP Cookies

These have a great malty flavour and a chewy texture. Perfect served with a cup of steaming hot cocoa.

MAKES: 18
BAKING TIME: 10–12 MINUTES

INGREDIENTS
125g butter, softened
100g sugar
1 egg, lightly beaten
1 teaspoon vanilla extract
5 tablespoons chocolate malt powder
100g plain flour
50g rolled oats

COOKIE TIP
To prevent baking paper slipping off baking sheets, sprinkle the baking sheet with a few drops of water beforehand.

1. Preheat the oven to 190°C/375°F/Gas mark 5. Line two baking sheets with non-stick baking paper.
2. Cream the butter and sugar together until light and fluffy. Beat in the egg and vanilla. Sift the chocolate malt powder and flour together and beat into the creamed mixture along with the oats until all the ingredients are well combined.
3. Drop heaped teaspoons of the dough onto the baking sheets, spacing well apart. Bake in the centre of the oven until just golden, 10–12 minutes. The lower baking sheet may need slightly longer. Leave the cookies to cool on the baking sheets for a few minutes, then transfer to a wire rack to cool completely.

SPICY BUTTERMILK Cookies

The mixed spice and tangy buttermilk in these cookies lends a sweet and gentle kick.

MAKES: 20
BAKING TIME: 10–15 MINUTES

INGREDIENTS
6 tablespoons butter, softened
150g sugar
150ml buttermilk
225g plain flour
½ teaspoon bicarbonate of soda
2 teaspoons mixed spice

1. Preheat the oven to 200°C/400°F/Gas mark 6. Lightly grease two baking sheets.
2. Cream the butter and sugar together in a bowl until light and fluffy. Beat in the buttermilk. Sift the flour, bicarbonate of soda and spice together and beat into the creamed mixture.
3. Drop rounded tablespoons of the dough onto the baking sheets, spacing well apart as the cookies will almost double in size.
4. Bake until golden, 10–15 minutes. Cool on the baking sheets for a few minutes before transferring to a wire rack to cool completely.

COOKIE TIP
If you prefer not to use buttermilk, yogurt is a very good substitute.

BASIC SPRITZ Cookies

Spritz cookies are a firm family favourite and perfect for popping in the mouth at any time. The name derives from the German verb spritzen, meaning 'squirt' or to 'spray'.

MAKES: **24–30**
BAKING TIME: **8–10 MINUTES**

INGREDIENTS
125g butter, softened
100g icing sugar
1 egg
½ teaspoon vanilla extract
250g plain flour
Coloured sugar crystals for decoration

1. Preheat the oven to 200°C/400°F/Gas mark 6. Lightly grease two baking sheets.
2. Cream the butter and sugar together until light and fluffy. Beat in the egg and vanilla. Fold in the flour.
3. If using a cookie press, chill the dough for about 30 minutes until firm but not hard. Press the cookies on to baking sheets. If you do not have a cookie press you can pipe the cookies, but do not chill the dough first.
4. Decorate with coloured sugar crystals and bake until lightly golden, about 8–10 minutes. Cool on the baking sheets for a few minutes before transferring to a wire rack to cool completely.

COOKIE TIP
Cool cookies on wire racks without touching each other to keep them from sticking together.

CHOCOLATE MINT Creams

A wonderful combination of crisp mint and warm sweet chocolate. If you prefer you could substitute the peppermint essence for orange essence to make Chocolate Orange Creams.

1. Cream the butter and sugar together until light and fluffy. Sift together the flour and cocoa powder and beat in until smooth. Form into a 5cm thick log and chill for 1 hour.
2. Preheat the oven to 190°C/375°F/Gas mark 5. Lightly grease two baking sheets. Cut the log into slices 5mm thick and arrange well apart on baking sheets. Bake until just firm, about 8 minutes.
3. Leave the cookies to cool on the baking sheets for a few minutes before transferring to a wire rack to cool completely.
4. To make the filling, place the cream in a mixing bowl and beat in the icing sugar. Add peppermint essence to taste.
5. Sandwich pairs of cookies together with the filling. Store in a cool place for up to three days.

MAKES: 18
BAKING TIME: 8 MINUTES

INGREDIENTS

175g butter, softened
50g sugar
200g plain flour
2 tablespoons unsweetened cocoa powder

FILLING

2 tablespoons milk or single cream
100g icing sugar
½–1 teaspoon peppermint essence

CHOCOLATE & PISTACHIO Fingers

Softer than normal shortbread these cookies are good served with tea or coffee.

MAKES: 12
BAKING TIME: 15 MINUTES

INGREDIENTS
200g unsalted butter
90g golden caster sugar
250g cups plain flour
50g plain cocoa powder
25g shelled pistachio nuts, roughly chopped
Plain cocoa powder for dusting

1. Preheat the oven to 180°C/350°F/Gas mark 4. Line a shallow square 18cm pan with baking paper.
2. Cream the butter and sugar together until light and fluffy. Sift together the flour and cocoa powder. Add to the butter mixture and work in using your hands until the mixture is smooth. Add the pistachios and knead until soft and pliable.
3. Press the mixture into the tin and smooth the top using the back of a tablespoon. Prick with a fork and mark into bars.
4. Bake in the oven for about 15 minutes. Do not allow to become too brown or the cookies will taste bitter.
5. Allow to cool slightly then cut through the marked sections and remove from the tin. Cool on a wire rack and dust sparingly with cocoa powder.

HONEY & LEMON Cookies

To make these cookies more attractive, you could use star-shaped cutters to give a more sophisticated finish.

MAKES: 16
BAKING TIME: 10–12 MINUTES

INGREDIENTS
Generous 250g plain flour
1 teaspoon bicarbonate of soda
50g sugar
Grated rind and juice of 1 lemon
125g butter
5 tablespoons honey

FILLING
4 tablespoons butter, softened
75g icing sugar
2 tablespoons honey
2 teaspoons lemon juice

1. Sift the flour and bicarbonate of soda into a bowl. Stir in the sugar and lemon rind. Blend in the butter until the mixture resembles fine breadcrumbs.

2. Heat the honey and lemon juice in a small pan until very runny but not too hot. Pour into the flour mixture and mix to form a soft dough. Chill for 30 minutes or until firm enough to handle. Preheat the oven to 190°C/375°F/Gas mark 5. Lightly grease a baking sheet.

3. Roll the dough into small balls and arrange well spaced on the baking sheet. Flatten slightly with a knife. Bake until golden brown, 10–12 minutes.

4. Cool on the baking sheet for a few minutes before transferring to a wire rack to cool completely.

5. To make the filling, cream the butter and icing sugar together until light and fluffy. Beat in the honey and lemon juice. Sandwich the cookies together in pairs with the filling.

LADY GREY TEA Cookies

The unusual ingredient in these cookies is Lady Grey tea – similar to Earl Grey but with the addition of Seville orange and lemon peel.

MAKES: 18–20
BAKING TIME: 10–15 MINUTES

INGREDIENTS
80g unsalted butter, at room temperature
50g soft light brown sugar
1 tablespoon Lady Grey tea leaves
1 egg white
150g plain flour

TOPPING
Demerara sugar

1. Preheat the oven to 190°C/375°F/Gas mark 5. Line baking sheets with baking paper.

2. Put the butter and sugar into a bowl and beat together until creamy. Stir in the tea leaves.

3. Beat in the egg white. Fold in the flour to make a soft but not sticky dough. On a lightly floured surface roll into a cylinder. Flatten slightly to make a cross section that looks like a finger biscuit with rounded ends. Wrap carefully in clingfilm and chill until firm enough to slice.

4. Cut into thin slices and place on the prepared baking sheets. Sprinkle each biscuit with demerara sugar. Bake in the oven for 10–15 minutes until lightly browned.

COOKIE TIP
Store delicate cookies between sheets of greaseproof paper for safe keeping.

NUTTY JAM Slices

Sticky and crunchy, these bite-sized slices are enjoyable to make and great for teatime snacking.

1. Lightly grease a baking sheet. Cream the butter and sugar together until light and fluffy. Beat in the egg yolk and almond extract. Work in the flour and ground almonds to form a firm dough. Add a little extra flour if the mixture is too soft.
2. Divide the dough in half and roll each into a log about 25cm long. Place on the prepared sheet.
3. Lightly beat the egg white with a fork and brush over each log. Lightly crush the almonds and press on to the logs. Flatten each log slightly. Use the handle of a wooden spoon to press a channel down the centre of each log. Fill the hollows with jam. Chill for 30 minutes.
4. Preheat the oven to 180°C/350°F/Gas mark 4.
5. Bake the logs until pale golden brown, 10–12 minutes. Leave on the baking sheet until the jam has set but the dough is still warm. Cut diagonally into slices and transfer to a wire rack to cool completely.

MAKES: 20
BAKING TIME: 10–12 MINUTES

INGREDIENTS
4 tablespoons butter
50g sugar
1 egg, separated
1 teaspoon almond extract
100g plain flour
25g ground almonds
25g sliced almonds
Jam of your choice

COFFEE & CINNAMON Cookies

The cinnamon flavour and attractive crescent shape of these little cookies makes them perfect for serving at Christmas time.

MAKES: 40
BAKING TIME: 12 MINUTES

INGREDIENTS

1 tablespoon instant coffee granules
1 tablespoon boiling water
225g butter
165g sugar
1 tablespoon Kahlúa or other coffee-flavoured liqueur
400g plain flour
2 teaspoons ground cinnamon
30g icing sugar

1. Preheat the oven to 180°C/350°F/Gas mark 4. Lightly grease two baking sheets. Dissolve the coffee in 1 tablespoon boiling water.
2. Cream the butter and sugar together until pale and fluffy. Beat in the coffee and liqueur. Sift the flour and 1 teaspoon of the cinnamon together, then beat into the dough.
3. Take small amounts of the dough, each about the size of a walnut, and roll into balls. Shape each ball into a log, then curve it into a crescent. Space well apart on the baking sheets. Bake until golden, about 12 minutes. Cool on the baking sheets for 2–3 minutes, then transfer to a wire rack to cool completely.
4. Sift the icing sugar and remaining cinnamon together a few times to ensure that the sugar and spice are well mixed. Dust the cookies with the spiced sugar. Store in an airtight container for up to five days.

BUTTERSCOTCH Fingers

A variation on the Viennese finger these cookies have a delicious butterscotch flavour and a delightful crisp coating.

MAKES: 9
BAKING TIME: 8–10 MINUTES

INGREDIENTS
225g unsalted butter
125g soft dark brown sugar
1 egg white
225g plain flour

BUTTERSCOTCH CREAM
2 tablespoons butter
1 tablespoon cream
150g golden icing sugar, sifted

GLAZE
100g golden icing sugar

1. Preheat the oven to 180°C/350°F/Gas mark 4. Beat the butter and sugar together until light and fluffy. Beat in the egg white. Stir in the flour and mix well.

2. Spoon the mixture into a piping bag fitted with a 1cm star tip and pipe eighteen 9cm long fingers on lightly greased baking sheets.

3. Bake for about 8–10 minutes or until lightly browned. Cool on a wire rack.

4. To make the glaze, put the icing sugar into a small bowl and add enough water to mix to a pouring consistency. Using a pastry brush, spread the glaze over each biscuit and allow to dry.

5. To make the filling, put the ingredients into a bowl and beat together until smooth. Sandwich the biscuits together with a little of the butterscotch cream.

COOKIE TIP
Make sure you allow the glaze to dry and the filling to set before storing in an airtight container.

ALMOND & VANILLA FUDGE Crumbles

Crumbly almond cookies with a crunchy topping have the surprise addition of tiny pieces of fudge.

MAKES: 24
BAKING TIME: 10–12 MINUTES

INGREDIENTS
200g self-raising flour
Pinch of salt
125g unsalted butter
100g soft light brown sugar
1 egg
1 teaspoon almond extract
50g ground almonds
50g vanilla cream fudge, finely diced

TOPPING
2 tablespoons flaked almonds, crumbled
2 tablespoons demerara sugar

1. Sift the flour and salt into a bowl. Blend in the butter. Add all the remaining ingredients (except those for the topping) and mix to a fairly firm dough. Wrap in clingfilm. Chill for 15 minutes.

2. Preheat the oven to 190°C/375°F/Gas mark 5. Divide the dough into 24 pieces and place, slightly apart on baking sheets lined with baking paper.

3. To make the topping: mix together the flaked almonds and demerara sugar and sprinkle a little on top of each cookie, pressing down lightly using the back of a spoon.

4. Bake in the oven for about 10–12 minutes until turning golden at the edges.

5. Remove from the oven and allow to cool for 5 minutes before removing to a wire rack.

Gypsy Creams

A crisp chocolate oat cookie encases a creamy chocolate filling in these hearty, classic and wholesome sandwich cookies.

MAKES: 10
BAKING TIME: 20 MINUTES

INGREDIENTS
4 tablespoons butter, softened
50g white vegetable fat
50g sugar
100g plain flour
50g rolled oats
1 tablespoon plain cocoa powder

FILLING
4 tablespoons butter, softened
75g icing sugar
2 tablespoons plain cocoa powder

1. Preheat the oven to 180°C/350°F/Gas mark 4. Lightly grease a baking sheet.

2. Cream the butter, fat and sugar together until light and fluffy. Beat in the remaining ingredients.

3. Roll the dough into small balls and place on the baking sheet. Flatten with a fork dipped in hot water. Bake until golden, about 20 minutes. Let cool on the baking sheet.

4. To make the filling, cream the butter until fluffy, then gradually beat in the icing sugar and cocoa powder. Sandwich the cookies together in pairs with the filling

TROPICAL FRUIT Cookies

Soft cookies packed with tropical fruit and topped with coconut icing.

MAKES: 16–18
BAKING TIME: 12 MINUTES

INGREDIENTS
125g butter
70g caster sugar
1 egg
150g self-raising flour
50g ground almonds
250g pack ready-to-eat tropical fruit mix, chopped

FROSTING
100g icing sugar
2–3 tablespoons coconut cream

1. Preheat the oven to 180°C/350°F/Gas mark 4. Put the butter and sugar into a bowl and beat together until creamy. Beat in the egg.

2. Stir in the flour, ground almonds and fruit. Place spoonfuls of the mixture 5cm apart on a non-stick baking sheet.

3. Bake in the oven for about 12 minutes or until lightly browned. Cool on a wire rack.

4. To make the icing: sift the icing sugar into a bowl. Add the coconut cream and mix until thick but not too runny. Spoon over the cookies and leave to set.

COOKIE TIP
Only store one kind of cookie in a container. If you mix crisp and soft cookies they will all go soft and end up tasting the same.

FRUITY OAT Bites

These are perfect as a healthy afternoon snack as the dried fruit will give long-lasting energy.

MAKES: 10
BAKING TIME: 20–25 MINUTES

INGREDIENTS
150g butter
75g soft light brown sugar
75g honey
175g muesli
75g rolled oats
100g chopped dried apricots
100g chopped dried apple
100g chopped dried mango

1. Preheat the oven to 190°C/375°F/Gas mark 5. Lightly grease a 20 x 20cm square tin and line the base with non-stick baking paper.
2. Melt the butter, sugar, and honey together in a saucepan, stirring until well combined. Remove from the heat and stir in the muesli, oats, apricots, apple and mango.
3. Press the mixture into the prepared cake tin. Bake for 20–25 minutes.
4. Allow to cool for a few minutes in the tin, then cut into bars. Allow to cool completely in the tin before serving. Store in an airtight container for up to two weeks.

LUNCHBOX

CHOC CHIP & MIXED NUT Cookies

A classic recipe for all the family that produces a chewy, melt-in-the-mouth cookie, just like Grandma used to make.

MAKES: 10–12
BAKING TIME: 15–18 MINUTES

INGREDIENTS
225g butter, softened
165g sugar
150g soft brown sugar
2 eggs
1 teaspoon vanilla extract
255g plain flour
1 teaspoon bicarbonate of soda
175g plain or milk chocolate chips
75g mixed nuts (walnuts, pecans, almonds, hazelnuts etc.), chopped

1. Preheat the oven to 160°C/325°F/Gas mark 3. Lightly grease two baking sheets.

2. Cream the butter and sugars together until light and fluffy. Beat in the eggs and vanilla. Sift the flour with the bicarbonate of soda and beat into the mixture. Add the chocolate chips and nuts and stir until well combined.

3. Drop large rounded tablespoons of the dough on to the baking sheets, five or six per sheet, well spaced as the cookies will spread.

4. Bake until golden, 15–18 minutes. Cool on the baking sheets for a few minutes before transferring to a wire rack to cool completely.

COOKIE TIP
Only grease the baking sheets when the recipe instructs you to. Otherwise the cookies may spread too much and become flat.

ORANGE & PEANUT BUTTER Cookies

The combination of zesty orange and rich peanut butter in this recipe makes for a fresh yet wholesome, tasty cookie.

MAKES: 24
BAKING TIME: 18–20 MINUTES

INGREDIENTS
125g butter, softened
100g sugar
1 egg, lightly beaten
75g peanut butter
Grated rind of 1 small orange
50ml orange juice
300g plain flour
1 teaspoon baking powder

1. Preheat the oven to 180°C/350°F/Gas mark 4. Lightly grease two baking sheets.
2. Cream the butter and sugar together until light and fluffy. Beat in the egg, peanut butter, orange rind and juice. Sift the flour and baking powder together and beat into the mixture.
3. Drop rounded tablespoons of the dough, spaced well apart on to the baking sheets. Flatten slightly with the back of a spoon.
4. Bake until golden, 18–20 minutes. Cool on the baking sheets for a few minutes before transferring to a wire rack to cool completely.

COOKIE TIP
For even baking, always bake cookies on the middle rack of your oven.

TRADITIONAL CHOC CHIP Cookies

Enjoy the contrast of white and plain chocolate chips in this delicious twist on everyone's favourite cookie.

MAKES: 14
BAKING TIME: 12–15 MINUTES

INGREDIENTS
150g plain chocolate chips
150g white chocolate chips
140g butter
150g sugar
1 egg
½ teaspoon vanilla extract
200g plain flour
1 teaspoon baking powder

1. Preheat the oven to 180°C/350°F/Gas mark 4 . Lightly grease two baking sheets.

2. Cream the butter and sugar together until pale and fluffy. Beat in the egg and the vanilla. Sift the flour and baking powder together and beat into the mixture. Add the chocolate chips and stir until well combined.

3. Drop 5–6 rounded tablespoons of the dough on to each baking sheet, spacing well apart, as the cookies will almost double in size.

4. Bake until golden, 12–15 minutes. Cool on the baking sheet for 2–3 minutes, then transfer to a wire rack to cool completely. Store in an airtight container for up to five days.

COOKIE TIP

Never drop cookies on to a hot baking sheet. Use two baking sheets if instructed to, or cool the sheet in between batches.

OATMEAL CHOC CHIP Cookies

For an old-fashioned, coarser texture, be sure to use rolled oats. However, if you prefer a smoother cookie, use instant oats.

MAKES: 10–12
BAKING TIME: 8–10 MINUTES

INGREDIENTS
150g plain flour
1 teaspoon baking powder
175g unsalted butter, softened
100g soft dark brown sugar
100g sugar
1 large egg, at room temperature
2 teaspoons vanilla extract
250g rolled oats
75g plain chocolate chips

1. Preheat the oven to 190°C/375°F/Gas mark 5. Lightly grease two baking sheets.
2. In a large bowl, stir together the flour and baking powder.
3. In a large mixing bowl and using a hand-held electric mixer, cream the butter and sugars together until light and fluffy. Add the egg and beat until combined. Stir in the vanilla. With the mixer on low speed or using a wooden spoon, gradually add the flour mixture until combined. Stir in the oats and the chocolate chips.
4. Drop rounded tablespoonfuls of the dough, well spaced apart on to the baking sheets. Leave space between each one for spreading. Flatten each cookie slightly with the back of the spoon. Bake until golden for 12–15 minutes.
5. Remove the cookies from the baking sheets to a wire rack and cool.

GINGER & DATE SANDWICH Cookies

Ginger and date makes for a great combination, however, you might like to replace the filling with raisins or even dried apricots instead of dates.

MAKES: 14
BAKING TIME: 12–15 MINUTES

INGREDIENTS
125g butter
100g sugar
1 tablespoon golden syrup
225g plain flour
1 teaspoon ground ginger
½ teaspoon baking powder

FILLING
100g stoned dates
50g sugar
75ml water

1. Preheat the oven to 190°C/375°F/Gas mark 5. Lightly grease two baking sheets.

2. Place the butter, sugar and syrup in a pan and heat gently, stirring until the butter melts. Remove from the heat. Sift the flour, ginger and baking powder together and stir into the butter mixture to form a dough.

3. Roll the dough into small balls and arrange on the baking sheets. Flatten slightly with a knife. Bake until golden, 12–15 minutes. Cool on a wire rack.

4. To make the filling, chop the dates. Place in a pan with the sugar and water. Heat gently, stirring, until the sugar dissolves. Bring to the boil, then reduce the heat and cook gently for about 15 minutes until the mixture reduces to a thick, spreadable paste. Remove from the heat and let cool.

5. Use the date mixture to sandwich the ginger cookies together in pairs. Store in an airtight container for up to four days.

CHERRY & CHOCOLATE NUT Slices

Although macadamia nuts taste wonderful alongside the cherries, hazelnuts would work equally well.

MAKES: 9

INGREDIENTS
200g plain chocolate
125g butter
175g golden syrup
350g gingersnap biscuits
125g glacé cherries
100g roughly chopped, toasted macadamia nuts

1. Roughly chop the chocolate and butter and place in a large bowl with the golden syrup. Melt by microwaving on medium for 2 minutes or by setting the bowl over a pan of simmering water.

2. Place half the gingersnaps in a food processor and process to fine crumbs. Roughly chop the remaining cookies and add both to the melted chocolate mixture. Halve the cherries and add with the nuts to the chocolate mixture. Combine thoroughly so that the biscuits, cherries, and nuts are coated with chocolate.

3. Line a 20 x 20cm loose-based square cake tin with non-stick baking paper. Spoon in the chocolate mixture and leave to set in the refrigerator for 2 hours. Remove from the tin, peel off the paper and cut into slices.

LEMON Thins

The tangy cream cheese of the filling contrasts beautifully with the zesty lemon of this cookie.

MAKES: 20
BAKING TIME: 8 MINUTES

INGREDIENTS
175g plain flour
3½ tablespoons cornflour
125g butter
50g icing sugar
Grated rind of ½ lemon
1 tablespoon lemon juice

FILLING
100g cream cheese
50g icing sugar
60g lemon curd

1. Preheat the oven to 200°C/400°F/Gas mark 6. Lightly grease two baking sheets. Sift the flour and cornflour into a mixing bowl. Cut the butter into small pieces and blend into the flour until the mixture resembles fine breadcrumbs.
2. Stir in the icing sugar and lemon rind. Add the lemon juice, then bring the mixture together with your hands to form a soft dough. Chill for 20 minutes.
3. On a lightly floured surface, roll out the dough as thin as possible and cut into rounds with a 5cm cookie cutter. Arrange on the baking sheets and bake until crisp and golden, about 8 minutes. Cool on the baking sheets for 2–3 minutes, then transfer to a wire rack to cool completely.
4. For the filling, beat together the cream cheese, icing sugar and lemon curd. Sandwich together pairs of cookies with the filling. Store in an airtight container in a cool place for up to three days.

COOKIE TIP
Baked and uncooked shaped cookies can be frozen for up to two months. Thaw baked cookies at room temperature and bake uncooked ones from frozen.

CARAMELITAS

The unbeatable combination of chocolate and caramel makes these bars a firm favourite.

MAKES: 20
BAKING TIME: 20–25 MINUTES

INGREDIENTS
200g rolled oats
200g plain flour
1 teaspoon bicarbonate of soda
300g soft light brown sugar
½ teaspoon salt
225g unsalted butter, melted
300g plain chocolate, roughly chopped
100g pecan nuts, lightly toasted and roughly chopped
250ml caramel sauce (or Dulce de Leche)

1. Preheat the oven to 180°C/350°F/Gas mark 4. Base line a 30 x 30cm shallow baking tin with baking paper.
2. Put the oats, flour, bicarbonate of soda, sugar and salt into a bowl and mix together. Add the butter and mix well. Spread half of the mixture in the base of the prepared tin. Press out evenly using the back of a spoon.
3. Bake in the oven for 10 minutes. Remove and sprinkle the chocolate and nuts evenly over the surface. Drizzle the caramel sauce evenly over the top. Sprinkle the reserved oat mixture on top and press gently with the back of a spoon.
4. Bake in the oven for 20–25 minutes until golden brown.
5. Leave in the tin to cool completely and cut into bars to serve.

COOKIE TIP

You can always vary nuts in recipes to suit personal taste. Pecans could be substituted with walnuts and almonds with hazelnuts for example.

SNICKERDOODLES

A soft traditional cookie, with a funny name, originating from 19th-century New England.

MAKES: 36
BAKING TIME: 8–10 MINUTES

INGREDIENTS
175g butter, softened
225g sugar
1 egg
1 teaspoon vanilla extract
300g plain flour
1 teaspoon cream of tartar
½ teaspoon bicarbonate of soda

COATING
1 tablespoon sugar
1 teaspoon ground cinnamon

COOKIE TIP
You could also try making wholemeal snickerdoodles by substituting 1 cup wholemeal flour for 1 cup of the plain flour.

1. Preheat the oven to 200°C/400°F/Gas mark 6. Lightly grease two baking sheets.
2. Cream the butter and the sugar together until light and fluffy. Beat in the egg and vanilla. Sift the flour, cream of tartar and bicarbonate of soda together and blend into the butter mixture to form a soft dough.
3. Break off pieces of the dough about the size of a small walnut and roll into balls. Mix the 1 tablespoon sugar and cinnamon together and roll each ball in the cinnamon sugar. Arrange on the baking sheets, allowing room for the cookies to spread.
4. Bake until pale golden, about 8–10 minutes. Transfer to a wire rack to cool.

SPICED Pretzels

With a lovely spicy flavour and unusual shape, these pretzels are sure to impress guests when offered as a savoury snack at a drinks party or impromptu get-together.

MAKES: 30
BAKING TIME: 18–20 MINUTES

INGREDIENTS
200g plain flour
½ teaspoon baking powder
Pinch of salt
6 tablespoons butter
1 tablespoon curry paste
50ml boiling water
Beaten egg, to glaze

1. Preheat the oven to 180°C/350°F/Gas mark 4. Lightly grease two baking sheets.
2. Sift the flour, baking powder and salt into a mixing bowl and blend in the butter until the mixture resembles fine bread crumbs. Stir the curry paste into 50ml boiling water, then add to the flour mixture and mix to form a soft dough.
3. Knead on a lightly floured surface until smooth. Divide into 30 pieces and roll each piece into a strand about 20cm long. Twist into a pretzel shape by making a round, then twisting the ends around each other to form a curved letter 'B'. Press into position to secure and place on the baking sheets.
4. Brush the pretzels with beaten egg. Bake until golden, 18–20 minutes. Carefully transfer to a wire rack to cool.
5. Store in an airtight container for one to two weeks.

SAVOURY Whirls

You can leave these plain or top with a selection of olives, anchovies, marinated peppers, nuts or sun-dried tomatoes.

MAKES: 15
BAKING TIME: 12–15 MINUTES

INGREDIENTS

125g butter, softened
1 clove garlic, crushed
2 tablespoons sour cream
150g plain flour
½ teaspoon paprika
Salt and freshly ground black pepper

1. Preheat the oven to 190°C/375°F/Gas mark 5. Lightly grease two baking sheets.
2. Cream the butter until soft, then beat in the garlic, sour cream, flour, paprika and seasoning. Mix to form a smooth paste.
3. Spoon into a piping bag fitted with a large star nozzle and pipe rosettes on to the baking sheets.
4. Bake until golden, 12–15 minutes. Cool on the baking sheets for a few minutes before transferring to a wire rack to cool completely.

COOKIE TIP

Always measure ingredients accurately. Use glass measuring jugs for liquid ingredients as it is more accurate to see the level of liquid.

SAVOURY PALMIER Cookies

These cookies are so versatile – spread them with whatever filling you choose. A little cheese sprinkled over the olives works well.

MAKES: 20
BAKING TIME: 15–18 MINUTES

INGREDIENTS

250g ready-made puff pastry, thawed if frozen
2 tablespoons pesto
50g stoned black olives, finely chopped

1. Preheat the oven to 200°C/400°F/Gas mark 6. Roll out the pastry on a lightly floured surface to form a 25 x 30cm rectangle. Trim the edges with a sharp knife.
2. Spread the pesto in a thin layer all over the pastry, taking care to go right to the edges. Sprinkle with the chopped olives. With the long side facing you, fold about 7.5cm of the shorter sides of the pastry so that they reach about halfway toward the centre. Fold again so that they just meet in the centre. Lightly dampen the pastry with a little water and fold again in half down the centre.
3. Using a sharp knife, cut the roll into about 20 thin slices and arrange cut-side down, well spaced, on the baking sheets.
4. Bake for 10 minutes, then turn them over and bake until golden and crisp, 5–8 minutes. Transfer to a wire rack to cool.

COOKIE TIP

Palmiers are best served slightly warm, however, if this is not possible, room temperature is fine.

SESAME CHEESE Twists

These classic twists are a favourite at parties and look very professional – however, they are actually unbelievably easy to make!

MAKES: 14
BAKING TIME: 10–12 MINUTES

INGREDIENTS
100g Cheddar cheese
125g butter, softened
200g cups plain flour
Beaten egg, to glaze
2 tablespoons sesame seeds

1. Preheat the oven to 200°C/400°F/Gas mark 6. Lightly grease two baking sheets. Finely grate the cheese, using the fine grater attachment of a food processor.

2. Remove the grating disc and insert the metal mixing blade. Place the butter in the food processor with the cheese and process until pale and creamy. Add the flour and process until the mixture comes together to form a ball of dough.

3. Roll out the dough on a lightly floured surface to about 3mm thick. Cut into strips about 15cm long and 5cm wide. Take two strips at a time and twist together, pinching the ends.

4. Arrange on the baking sheets. Brush with beaten egg and sprinkle with sesame seeds. Bake until pale golden, 10–12 minutes. Let cool for a few minutes on the baking sheets, then transfer to a wire rack to cool completely. Store in an airtight container for up to one week.

CHEESE & TOMATO Bites

Serve these cheese-filled tomato cookies with pre-dinner drinks. Or why not pack a few into your lunchbox as a savoury snack at any time of day?

MAKES: 30
BAKING TIME: 10–12 MINUTES

INGREDIENTS
175g plain flour
½ teaspoon baking powder
6 tablespoons butter
1 teaspoon celery salt (optional)
2 tablespoons ketchup

FILLING
100g cream cheese
1 tablespoon snipped chives
Salt and freshly ground black pepper

1. Preheat the oven to 200°C/400°F/Gas mark 6. Lightly grease two baking sheets.
2. Place the flour and baking powder in a bowl. Blend in the butter until the mixture resembles fine breadcrumbs. Stir in the celery salt, then add the ketchup and mix to form a stiff dough.
3. Roll out on a lightly floured surface and cut into 2.5cm wafers with a knife or biscuit cutter. Arrange on the baking sheets. Bake until golden, 10–12 minutes. Cool on the baking sheets for a few minutes before transferring to a wire rack to cool completely.
4. Beat together the cream cheese and chives and season to taste. Use to sandwich two wafers together. The wafers will keep unfilled for up to one week in an airtight container; fill just prior to serving.

BLUE CHEESE & POPPY SEED Cookies

Great in a lunchbox these tasty cookies also make delightful cocktail snacks.

MAKES: 25–30
BAKING TIME: 10 MINUTES

INGREDIENTS
150g plain flour
100g butter at room temperature
75g mild full-fat soft blue cheese
2 tablespoons poppy seeds

1. Put the flour, butter and blue cheese into a bowl and mix well together. Place the mixture on clingfilm and shape into a cylinder 4cm in diameter. Chill until firm.

2. Preheat the oven to 180°C/350°F/Gas mark 4. Unwrap the dough and roll in the poppy seeds. Cut into slices and place 3cm apart on a non-stick baking sheet. Bake for about 10 minutes until lightly browned. Cool on a wire rack.

COOKIE TIP

Always chill cookie dough in the refrigerator when instructed to do so. This will make the dough easier to work with when you are cutting into slices ready to bake.

OAT Cakes

The oaty flavour and texture of these savoury treats works very well with cheese and chutney.

MAKES: 12
BAKING TIME: 15–20 MINUTES

INGREDIENTS
100g porridge oats
50g plain flour
1 teaspoon bicarbonate of soda
1 teaspoon sugar
Pinch of salt
4 tablespoons butter
1–2 tablespoons water

1. Preheat the oven to 180°C/350°F/Gas mark 4. Lightly grease a baking sheet.
2. Put the oats, flour, bicarbonate of soda, sugar and salt in a mixing bowl. Place the butter and 1–2 tablespoons water in a small saucepan and heat until the butter melts. Stir into the oat mixture and combine to form a dough.
3. Turn out onto a lightly floured surface and knead until the dough is no longer sticky, adding a little extra flour if necessary.
4. Roll out the dough until 7.5mm thick and cut out 7.5cm rounds with a biscuit cutter. Arrange on the baking sheet and bake until golden, 15–20 minutes. Remove to a wire rack to cool. Store in an airtight container for up to two weeks.

CHEWY TRAIL MIX Cookies

Healthy cookies that are truly delicious and will keep you going right till supper

MAKES: 30
BAKING TIME: 20 MINUTES

INGREDIENTS
200g butter, softened
180g soft light brown sugar
170g granulated sugar
4 tablespoons honey
2 eggs
2 teaspoons vanilla extract
350g plain flour
½ teaspoon baking powder
½ teaspoon bicarbonate of soda
1 teaspoon ground cinnamon
¼ teaspoon salt
90g unsalted cashew nuts, chopped
90g roughly chopped walnuts
130g pumpkin seeds
70g sunflower seeds
125g rolled oats
350g seedless raisins

1. Preheat the oven to 150°C/300°F/Gas mark 2. Use non-stick baking sheets or line baking sheets with baking paper.

2. Put the butter, sugars, honey, eggs and vanilla into a large bowl and beat well together. Sift together the flour, baking powder, bicarbonate of soda, cinnamon and salt. Mix into the butter mixture.

3. Stir in the cashews, walnuts, half the pumpkin seeds, sunflower seeds, oats and raisins. Take pieces of dough about the size of an apricot and roll into balls. Dip one side into the reserved pumpkin seeds, place on the baking sheet and flatten with the palm of your hand.

4. Bake in the oven for 20 minutes. Allow to cool slightly on the baking sheet before removing to a wire rack.

COOKIE TIP

Honey is a great storecupboard standby and will last with the lid screwed tightly for quite a while. However, if it has crystallized over time, stand the jar in a pan of hot water until it liquifies again.

CHEESY Crumbles

These chewy, cheesy bites are the perfect bite-sized snack.

MAKES: 20
BAKING TIME: 15 MINUTES

INGREDIENTS
115g Cheddar cheese
4 spring onions
25g walnuts
100g plain flour
1 teaspoon wholegrain Dijon mustard
6 tablespoons butter

1. Preheat the oven to 190°C/375°F/Gas mark 5. Grate the cheese coarsely into a bowl. Thinly slice the spring onions and finely chop the walnuts and stir into the cheese. Stir in the flour and mustard.
2. Melt the butter and add to the cheese mixture, stirring until well blended. Shape into 2.5cm balls and place on lightly greased baking sheets. Flatten slightly with a spatula.
3. Bake for about 15 minutes until golden brown. Leave to cool on the sheets for 2–3 minutes before transferring to a wire rack to cool completely. Best eaten warm or on the day they are made, but they can be stored in an airtight container in a cool place for up to three days.

BUTTER Cookies

Although this recipe for rough puff pastry is ideal for topping savoury meat pies, it also makes fabulous cookies.

MAKES: 10-12
BAKING TIME: 8–10 MINUTES

INGREDIENTS
225g plain flour
½ teaspoon salt
1 teaspoon baking powder
Pinch of bicarbonate of soda
175g unsalted butter
6 tablespoons cold buttermilk
1 tablespoon melted butter, for brushing

1. Sift the flour, salt, baking powder and bicarbonate of soda into a mixing bowl. Cut the butter into cubes, add to the flour, and blend together, using your fingertips until the mixture resembles coarse breadcrumbs.
2. Stir in half the buttermilk and begin mixing the dough together, adding just enough of the remaining buttermilk to make a soft dough. Turn the dough onto a floured surface and dust with flour. Roll the dough out to 2.5cm thick. Lift the dough from the surface and fold it in thirds. Give the dough a quarter turn. Flour the surface and dough again and reroll into a rectangle of the same thickness. Repeat the folding and turning.
3. Transfer the dough to a baking sheet lined with baking paper. Cover with clingfilm and chill, about 20 minutes.
4. Remove from the refrigerator and repeat the rolling and folding twice more. Roll a final time to a 2cm thick rectangle. Now either cut the dough into triangles or use a biscuit cutter to cut the dough into rounds.
5. Put the cut dough about 2.5cm apart on the paper-lined baking sheet. Cover with clingfilm and chill for at least 20 minutes.
6. Preheat the oven to 240°C/475°F/Gas mark 4. Brush the tops of the cookies with melted butter and transfer to the oven. Reduce the temperature to 190°C/375°F/Gas mark 5.
7. Bake until golden all over, 12–15 minutes. Let cool 5 minutes.

COOKIE TIP

The dough can be made ahead and refrigerated or frozen and then baked fresh to eat with soup, or for breakfast or with roast meat and gravy.

PIZZA Chunks

Although the ingredients may seem a little grown-up, these tasty crackers are a firm favourite with children.

MAKES: 24–30
BAKING TIME: 10–15 MINUTES

INGREDIENTS
180g plain flour
150g butter
20g grated Parmesan cheese
25g grated mature Cheddar cheese
1 tablespoon sun-dried tomato paste
25g sun-dried tomatoes, roughly chopped
1–2 teaspoons Italian dried mixed herbs
1 egg yolk
1 tablespoon water

1. Preheat the oven to 180°C/350°F/Gas mark 4. Put all the ingredients into a food processor and process, using the pulse button until the mixture just comes together.

2. Roll out the dough between sheets of baking paper, to a large rectangle shape.

3. Remove the top piece of baking paper and lift the dough, using the bottom paper, on to a baking sheet. Leave the bottom paper in place. Using a fork or pastry wheel, mark lightly into squares or bars.

4. Bake in the oven for about 10–15 minutes until lightly browned.

5. Cool on a wire rack on the baking paper and then break into pieces along the perforations.

COOKIE TIP

Always pay special attention when measuring flour for baking recipes – too much and your cookies will be too hard, and too little and your cookies will be flat.

KIDS' COOKIES

GIANT M&M Bites

These fun, giant cookies are perfect for packing in kids' lunchboxes as a special treat.

MAKES: 12
BAKING TIME: 8–10 MINUTES

INGREDIENTS
125g butter, softened
75g sugar
75g soft light brown sugar
1 egg
1 teaspoon vanilla extract
200g self-raising flour
100g peanut or chocolate M&Ms or sugar-coated chocolates

1. Preheat the oven to 190°C/375°F/Gas mark 5. Lightly grease two baking sheets.
2. Cream the butter and sugars together until light and fluffy. Beat in the egg and vanilla. Sift the flour and beat into the mixture. Add the M&Ms and stir until well combined.
3. Drop rounded tablespoons of the dough on to the baking sheets, spacing well apart as the cookies will almost double in size.
4. Bake until golden, 8–10 minutes. Cool on the baking sheets for a few minutes before transferring to a wire rack to cool completely. These are best eaten the day they are made.

COOKIE TIP
Always stir flour prior to measuring – flour settles as it sits and if you don't stir it you may end up adding too much to your cookies.

PEANUT BUTTER Cookies

If you prefer a soft, chewy cookie, bake only until the edges have browned slightly.

MAKES: 24
BAKING TIME: 10–12 MINUTES

INGREDIENTS
6 tablespoons butter
6 tablespoons sugar
150g crunchy peanut butter
1 egg
3 tablespoons golden syrup
175g plain flour
1 teaspoon baking powder

1. Preheat the oven to 180°C/350°F/Gas mark 4. Lightly grease two baking sheets.

2. Cream the butter and sugar together until pale and fluffy. Add the peanut butter, egg and golden syrup and beat until well combined.

3. Sift the flour with the baking powder and work into the mixture to form a soft dough. On a lightly floured surface, knead the dough lightly, then shape into a thick log. Cover with plastic wrap and let chill for 30 minutes.

4. Cut the dough into slices 5mm thick and space well apart on the baking sheets. Press a criss-cross pattern into the dough with the tines of a fork.

5. Bake until golden, 10–12 minutes. Let cool on the baking sheets for 2–3 minutes, then transfer to a wire rack to cool completely. Store in an airtight container for up to five days.

COOKIE TIP
Use smooth peanut butter if you prefer a creamier texture.

TEDDIES ON a Stick

Younger children will love these cute teddies and they are great to make for cake sales.

MAKES: 25
BAKING TIME: 8–10 MINUTES

INGREDIENTS

LIGHT DOUGH

180g plain flour
½ teaspoon ground cinnamon
¼ teaspoon bicarbonate of soda
50g butter
100g soft light brown sugar
2 tablespoons golden syrup
1 egg, beaten

DARK DOUGH

180g plain flour
½ teaspoon ground ginger
¼ teaspoon bicarbonate of soda
50g butter
90g soft dark brown sugar
2 tablespoons black treacle
1 egg, beaten

TO SERVE

Wooden lolly sticks
Plain and white chocolate chips

1. Preheat the oven to 190°C/375°F/Gas mark 5. Make up the dark and light dough in the same way.

2. Sift the flour, spice and bicarbonate of soda into a bowl. Blend in the butter and stir in the sugar. Warm the syrup or treacle in a small saucepan and add with the beaten egg to the flour mixture. Knead until smooth.

3. Roll out on a lightly floured surface and using a plain round 6cm cutter stamp out rounds from the light and dark dough. Place on baking sheets lined with baking paper. Insert a lolly stick into the base of each round.

4. Roll out the trimmings from each dough and using a plain round 2.5cm cutter stamp out two rounds for each cookie. Use light dough with dark face and vice versa. Place one round on each cookie for the nose. Cut the other in half and place on the face for the ears. Mark the nose with a knife.

5. Bake in the oven for 8–10 minutes. Remove and while still warm position the chocolate chips for eyes.

TUTTI FRUTTI Cookies

Packed full of fruit, these sweet cookies are adored by young and old alike.

MAKES: 24
BAKING TIME: 10–12 MINUTES

INGREDIENTS
125g butter, softened
100g sugar
1 egg, lightly beaten
Grated rind and juice of ½ orange
225g plain flour
50g mixed peel, chopped
50g glacé cherries, quartered
25g crystallized pineapple, chopped

1. Preheat the oven to 190°C/375°F/Gas mark 5. Lightly grease two baking sheets.

2. Cream the butter and sugar together until light and fluffy. Beat in the egg, orange juice and rind. Add the flour and beat into the mixture. Stir in the fruit.

3. Drop rounded tablespoons of the dough on to the baking sheets, spacing well apart as the cookies will almost double in size.

4. Bake until golden, 10–12 minutes. Cool on the baking sheets for a few minutes before transferring to a wire rack to cool completely.

COOKIE TIP
When making drop cookies, use a spoon from your daily cutlery – not a measuring spoon – to drop them. The deep bowl of a measuring spoon will make the dough harder to remove.

CHOCOLATE & VANILLA Whirls

For these cookies, the dough should be quite soft; you may find it easier to handle if you roll it out on non-stick baking paper. If it is too soft to roll, chill for 10–15 minutes to firm slightly.

MAKES: 30
BAKING TIME: 10–12 MINUTES

INGREDIENTS
175g butter
90g icing sugar
1 teaspoon vanilla extract
230g plain flour
2 tablespoons chocolate hazelnut spread, such as Nutella
1 tablespoon plain cocoa powder

1. Preheat the oven to 160°C/325°F/Gas mark 3. Lightly grease two baking sheets.

2. Cream the butter and icing sugar together until pale and fluffy. Beat in the vanilla.

3. Add the flour into the mixture and blend to form a soft dough. Divide the dough in half and work the chocolate hazelnut spread and cocoa powder into one half.

4. Roll each piece of dough on a lightly floured surface to a 15 x 20cm rectangle. Place one piece of dough on top of the other and press together lightly. Trim the edges and roll up lengthways like a Swiss roll. Cover and chill for 30 minutes.

5. Cut the dough into 5mm slices and space well apart on the baking sheets. Bake until golden, 10–12 minutes. Cool 2–3 minutes on the baking sheets, then transfer to a wire rack to cool completely.

ICE CREAM SANDWICH Cookies

Great to make in the school holidays – either keep the cookies in an airtight container and make fresh sandwiches each time with softened ice cream or make the sandwiches complete with ice cream and freeze.

MAKES: 10
BAKING TIME: 15 MINUTES

INGREDIENTS
115g unsalted butter at room temperature
115g caster sugar
1 egg, beaten
200g plain flour
25g plain cocoa powder, sifted
100g plain chocolate chips
Chocolate or vanilla ice cream

1. Preheat the oven to 180°C/350°F/Gas mark 4. Line a baking sheet with baking paper.

2. Cream the butter and sugar together and beat in the egg. Stir in the flour, cocoa and chocolate chips to make a firm dough. Roll out on non-stick baking paper. Cut into 20 rectangles each 7.5 x 6cm.

3. Place on the baking sheet. Bake in the oven for about 15 minutes. Cool.

4. To make the ice cream cookies spread two good spoonfuls of softened ice cream on a cookie and press a second cookie on top. Squeeze so the filling reaches the edges. Eat straightaway or wrap individually in foil and freeze. May be kept up to two weeks in the freezer.

COOKIE TIP
You can use any flavour of ice cream for these sweet treats: choc chip, coconut, raspberry ripple, praline etc.

DOMINO Cookies

Make chocolate-flavoured dominoes by substituting 2 tablespoons of cocoa powder for the same amount of flour. Pipe dots and lines with white icing.

MAKES: 14
BAKING TIME: 8–10 MINUTES

INGREDIENTS
6 tablespoons butter, softened
75g sugar
1 egg
1 teaspoon vanilla extract
200g plain flour
50g ground rice
25g plain chocolate for decoration

1. Cream the butter and sugar together until light and fluffy. Beat in the egg and vanilla. Sift the flour and ground rice together and beat in to form a soft dough. Chill for 30 minutes.

2. Preheat the oven to 180°C/350°F/Gas mark 4. Lightly grease a baking sheet. Roll out the dough on a lightly floured surface to about 5mm thick and cut out rectangles measuring about 5 x 7.5cm. Arrange slightly spaced on the baking sheet.

3. Bake until pale golden, 10–12 minutes. Cool on the baking sheet for a few minutes before transferring to a wire rack to cool completely.

4. To decorate, melt the chocolate in a microwave or in a bowl set over a saucepan of hot water. Spoon into a piping bag fitted with a small writing nozzle. Pipe domino dots and lines on to the cookies and leave to set.

5. Store in an airtight container for up to one week.

NEAPOLITAN Cookies

Children love making these simple but fun multicoloured cookies.

MAKES: 24
BAKING TIME: 8–10 MINUTES

INGREDIENTS
175g butter, softened
150g sugar
1 teaspoon vanilla extract
250g plain flour
1 tablespoon cocoa powder
1 teaspoon milk
½ teaspoon strawberry flavouring
Few drops red food colouring (optional)

1. Preheat the oven to 190°C/375°F/Gas mark 5. Lightly grease two baking sheets.

2. Cream the butter and sugar together until pale and fluffy. Beat in the vanilla. Add the flour and mix to form a smooth, soft dough. Divide into three equal portions.

3. Beat the cocoa powder and milk into one portion and mix to a smooth dough. Mix the strawberry flavouring and red food colouring, if using, into another portion. Leave the third portion plain.

4. Shape the chocolate-flavoured portion into a sausage, then flatten to form a 5 x 25cm rectangle. Repeat with the plain portion and place on top of the chocolate portion. Finally, repeat with the strawberry portion and stack on top.

5. Cut the bar into about 24 slices and lay flat on the baking sheets, allowing room for the cookies to spread. Bake until just firm, 8–10 minutes. Cool on the baking sheets for a few minutes before transferring to a wire rack to cool completely.

COOKIE TIP

If you only have one baking sheet, make sure you cool it well between batches.

MERINGUE Critters

Older kids can have fun making these meringue treats whilst younger ones can help Mum and eat the results!

MAKES: 14–16
BAKING TIME: 45–60 MINUTES

INGREDIENTS
2 egg whites
100g caster sugar
TO DECORATE
Icing sugar
Liquorice
Flaked almonds
Coloured sugar sprinkles
Assorted sweets for decoration

COOKIE TIP
When making meringue it is easier to separate the eggs when they are cold—but let the whites come to room temperature before using.

1. Put the egg whites in a bowl and beat until they form firm peaks. Gradually beat in the sugar a spoonful at a time. Beat for 15 seconds after each addition. Continue beating until very thick and shiny.
2. Preheat the oven to 150°C/300°F/Gas mark 2. Line a baking sheet with baking paper.
3. Pipe critters as described below and bake in the oven for 45–60 minutes until dry and crisp.

Mice Spoon meringue into a piping bag fitted with a 2.5cm plain nozzle. Pipe a blob 1cm high. Then pipe over this to make a shape like a mouse, taking pressure off the bag at the end to make a pointed nose. Place two silver balls or tiny pieces of sweets for the eyes, and a liquorice tail.

Hedgehogs Spoon meringue into a pastry bag fitted with a 2.5cm fluted star nozzle and pipe as above. Add on eyes and place flaked almonds in the back for the spines.

Snails Spoon the meringue into a piping bag fitted with a 1cm plain nozzle. Pipe a small blob for the head and then pipe a spiral for the snail shell. Make feelers and eyes from pieces of sweets or liquorice.

Snakes Fill a pastry bag as for snails and pipe wavy lines about 13cm long. Bake and allow to cool. When cold, glaze the meringue with a little icing sugar and water and sprinkle with coloured sugar sprinkles.

CHOCOLATE CARAMEL Slices

These delicious marbled slices are perfect for any special occasion.

MAKES: 12
BAKING TIME: 25 MINUTES

INGREDIENTS
125g butter, softened
50g sugar
150g plain flour
3 tablespoons cornflour

FILLING
6 tablespoons butter
50g soft light brown sugar
1 tablespoon golden syrup
400g tinned sweetened condensed milk

TOPPING
100g plain or milk chocolate
1 tablespoon butter
25g white chocolate

1. Preheat the oven to 180°C/350°F/Gas mark 4. Grease an 20 x 20cm square cake tin and line the base with non-stick baking paper.

2. Cream the butter and sugar together until light and fluffy. Sift together the flour and cornflour and mix in to form a smooth dough. Press the mixture into the base of the tin. Bake until just golden and firm, about 25 minutes.

3. To make the filling, combine the ingredients in a saucepan and heat gently, stirring until the sugar dissolves. Bring slowly to the boil and boil the mixture gently for about 5 minutes, stirring constantly with a wooden spoon until thickened. Pour evenly over the cookie base.

4. To make the topping, melt the plain or milk chocolate in a bowl set over a saucepan of hot water. Stir in the butter. Spread over the caramel filling. Melt the white chocolate in the same way. Spoon into a piping bag and pipe squiggles over the darker chocolate. (Alternatively, drizzle the white chocolate from a spoon.) Swirl with a skewer to create a marbled effect and leave to set. Serve cut into squares.

ICEBOX SUGAR Cookies

The chill-and-bake nature of these cookies means that you can make the dough well ahead of time and bake the cookies as you need them.

MAKES: 45
BAKING TIME: 8–10 MINUTES

INGREDIENTS
275g butter, softened
200g sugar
1 egg
1 teaspoon vanilla extract
350g plain flour
Coloured sugar sprinkles for decoration

1. Cream the butter and sugar together until pale and fluffy. Beat in the egg and vanilla. Add the flour and mix to form a soft dough.
2. Shape into a log about 5cm thick. Spread the sugar sprinkles on a sheet of non-stick baking paper and roll the log in the sugar until well coated.
3. Wrap the log in another sheet of baking paper and chill until firm. At this point the dough can be stored in the refrigerator for up to one week, or placed in a plastic bag and frozen for up to two months.
4. When ready to bake, preheat the oven to 190°C/375°F/Gas mark 5. Lightly grease two baking sheets. Cut the log into slices 3mm thick and arrange carefully on the baking sheets, leaving enough room for the cookies to spread.
5. Bake until just firm, 8–10 minutes. Cool on the baking sheets for a few minutes before transferring to a wire rack to cool completely.

COOKIE TIP
Preheat the oven for at least 10 minutes prior to baking.

ICED SPRINKLE Cookies

Fun and colourful, you could also decorate these cookies with melted chocolate instead of the icing. Use chocolate sprinkles, too.

MAKES: 18–24
BAKING TIME: 8 MINUTES

INGREDIENTS
125g butter, softened
50g icing sugar
1 teaspoon vanilla extract
175g plain flour
2 tablespoons ground rice

ICING
100g icing sugar
1 tablespoon water or lemon juice
Coloured sugar sprinkles

1. Preheat the oven to 200°C/400°F/Gas mark 6.
2. Cream the butter and the icing sugar together until pale and fluffy. Beat in the vanilla. Add the flour and ground rice and mix to form a soft dough.
3. Place the dough between two sheets of cling film and roll out to about 3mm thick. Cut out cookies using a 5–7.5cm biscuit cutter and carefully transfer to the baking sheets.
4. Bake until crisp and golden, about 8 minutes. Cool on the baking sheets for a few minutes before transferring to a wire rack to cool completely.
5. Sift the icing sugar into a bowl and add enough water or lemon juice to mix to a smooth icing. Spread the icing over the cookies with a metal spatula and decorate with sugar sprinkles. Let icing set before serving.

COOKIE TIP
Always sift icing sugar prior to use to avoid clumping.

ROCKY ROAD Cookies

Rich cookies, with a strong coconut taste. Decorate them by dipping in chocolate or drizzling a little chocolate over the top.

MAKES: 20
BAKING TIME: 12 MINUTES

INGREDIENTS
225g plain flour
1 teaspoon baking powder
125g butter
100g sugar
1 egg
½ teaspoon vanilla extract

TOPPING
50g mini marshmallows
75g chopped walnuts
50g plain chocolate

1. Preheat the oven to 180°C/350°F/Gas mark 4. Lightly grease two baking sheets.
2. Sift the flour and baking powder together into a mixing bowl. In a separate bowl, cream the butter and sugar together until pale and fluffy. Beat in the egg and vanilla, then work in the flour mixture to form a soft dough.
3. Take small amounts of the dough, each about the size of a walnut, and roll into balls. Space well apart on the baking sheets and flatten slightly. Bake until just golden, about 12 minutes. Reduce the oven temperature to 160°C/325°F/Gas mark 3.
4. To make the topping: mix together the marshmallows and nuts. Melt the chocolate in a bowl set over a saucepan of gently simmering water, making sure the base of the bowl is not touching the water. Spread a little on top of each cookie and top with the marshmallow and nut mixture.
5. Return the cookies to the oven and bake 1–2 minutes until the marshmallow softens. Cool on the baking sheets for 2–3 minutes before transferring to a wire rack to cool completely.
6. Drizzle or pipe the remaining chocolate over the cookies.

WHITE CHOCOLATE & CHERRY Cookies

Make up a batch of these scrumptious cookies for when only something sweet will do. Just try not to eat them all at once as they're utterly irresistible!

MAKES: 18
BAKING TIME: 12–15 MINUTES

INGREDIENTS
125g white chocolate
125g unsalted butter, softened
125g caster sugar
1 egg
125g rolled oats
150g plain flour
½ teaspoon baking powder
75g dried cherries

1. Preheat the oven to 180°C/350°F/Gas mark 5 and grease two baking sheets. Chop the white chocolate into small chunks and set aside. Cream the butter and sugar together in a bowl until pale and fluffy. Beat in the egg, and then add the oats.

2. Sift the flour and baking powder over the mixture, and fold in. Stir in the white chocolate and cherries.

3. Drop dessertspoonfuls of the mixture on to the baking sheets, spacing them well apart. Flatten each one slightly and bake for 12–15 minutes, or until golden. Transfer to a wire rack to cool.

COOKIE TIP
Don't drop cookie dough on to a hot baking sheet as the cookies will spread too much.

CHOCOLATE THUMBPRINT Cookies

Kids love helping to bake these chocolate cookies. Using white chocolate to fill the well in each cookie gives a lovely colour contrast. Alternatively, try using peanut butter for a smooth, nutty flavour.

MAKES: 24
BAKING TIME: 10 MINUTES

INGREDIENTS
50g plain chocolate
4 tablespoons butter
50g white vegetable fat
50g sugar
175g plain flour
FILLING
75g plain, milk, or white chocolate

1. Melt the chocolate in a microwave or in a bowl set over a pan of hot water. Let cool.
2. Cream the butter, fat, and sugar together until light and fluffy. Beat in the melted chocolate, then the flour and mix to form a smooth dough. Chill for 30 minutes.
3. Preheat the oven to 180°C/350°F/Gas mark 4. Lightly grease a baking sheet. Shape the dough into 2.5cm balls and arrange well spaced on the baking sheet. Press your thumb into the centre of each ball to form a well.
4. Bake for 10 minutes. Cool for a few minutes on the baking sheet, then transfer to a wire rack to cool completely.
5. For the filling, melt the chocolate in a microwave or in a bowl set over a saucepan of hot water. Spoon or pipe into the centre of the cookies and let set.

SMILIES

Kids will love to make these cookies and they can show off their creative talents by making many different faces.

MAKES: 16
BAKING TIME: 8–10 MINUTES

INGREDIENTS

VANILLA MIX
125g butter
50g caster sugar
150g plain flour

CHOCOLATE MIX
125g butter
50g caster sugar
130g plain flour
2 tablespoons plain cocoa powder
2 tablespoons drinking chocolate

1. Preheat the oven to 180°C/350°F/Gas mark 4. For each flavour cream together the butter and sugar until light and fluffy. Gradually mix in the remaining ingredients until a soft dough is formed.

2. Roll out the vanilla mixture on a lightly floured board to 5mm thick. Using a 7.5cm plain cutter stamp out biscuit faces. Place on a non-stick or lightly greased baking sheet. Keep the trimmings.

3. Roll out the chocolate mixture in the same way and cut out mouths, eyes, noses and hair and gently place on the vanilla faces. Curve the mouths up for smilies – maybe one turned down for sad.

4. Then cut out chocolate faces and use vanilla trimmings for the features.

5. Bake in the oven for about 10–12 minutes.

COOKIE TIP

Dip cutters in flour as you go along to keep the dough from sticking to them and tearing the cookies. Re-roll as little as possible.

SNOWBALLS

Easy to make and very tasty to eat, these make a great Christmas gift.

MAKES: 12

INGREDIENTS
200g white chocolate
2 tablespoons butter
100g sweetened and tenderized coconut
100g leftover sponge cake, crumbled
Icing sugar

1. Break the chocolate into pieces and place in a bowl with the butter. Put over a saucepan of gently simmering water.
2. Put 50g of the coconut on to a plate. Put the remaining coconut into a bowl with the crumbled cake crumbs. Add the melted chocolate and mix to form a paste.
3. Work quite quickly while the mixture is still warm. Roll the mixture into balls about the size of a walnut and immediately roll in the reserved coconut.
4. Leave to set and then dredge liberally with icing sugar.

COOKIE TIP

Most icing sugar is blended with a small amount of cornflour to prevent major lumping. Even so, it's usually best to sift it prior to use.

HOLIDAY COOKIES

SWEETHEART Cookies

These pretty cookies make a delightful gift for a friend or relative. Why not present them in a small basket or giftbox?

MAKES: 8
BAKING TIME: 15–20 MINUTES

INGREDIENTS
225g butter
6 g icing sugar
1 teaspoon vanilla extract
30g cornflour
225g plain flour
150g plain chocolate

1. Preheat the oven to 180°C/ 350°F/Gas mark 4. Draw four heart shapes on two pieces of non-stick baking paper. Place ink-side down on two baking sheets.
2. Cream the butter and icing sugar together until pale and fluffy. Beat in the vanilla. Sift together the cornflour and flour, and beat into the mixture.
3. Place the dough in a large piping bag fitted with a star nozzle. Pipe heart shapes on to the baking paper following the line drawings.
4. Bake until pale gold, 15–20 minutes. Cool on the baking sheets for 2–3 minutes, then transfer to a wire rack to cool completely.
5. Melt the chocolate in a bowl set over a saucepan of gently simmering water. Cool slightly, then dip half of each heart in the chocolate to decorate. Store in an airtight container for up to four days.

LIPSMACKING KISS Cookies

The perfect Valentine's Day gift for that special someone.

MAKES: 20
BAKING TIME: 7–8 MINUTES

INGREDIENTS

115g butter, cut into cubes
225g plain flour
175g sugar
1 egg, beaten
300g red fondant icing
75g icing sugar
Red food colouring

1. Preheat the oven to 200°C/400°F/Gas mark 6. Draw a lip shape on to a piece of card, cut out and set aside to use as a template.
2. Blend the butter into the flour until the mixture resembles fine breadcrumbs. Stir in the sugar, egg and 1–2 tablespoons cold water to bind the mixture to a soft but not sticky dough. Chill for 20 minutes.
3. Roll out on a lightly floured surface to a 5mm thickness. Using the template, cut around it to make 20 kiss cookies. Space well apart on two baking sheets and bake for 7–8 minutes. Cool completely.
4. Roll out the fondant on a surface lightly dusted with icing sugar to a 3mm thickness and cut out 20 kisses using the template.
5. Sift the icing sugar and mix with 2 teaspoons water to a very thick paste. Add a little red food colouring to make a smooth, thick, pink glacé icing. Spoon into a paper piping bag and snip off the end. Pipe a few dots on each cookie. Lift the fondant kisses and place 1 on top of each cookie. Pipe a fine line of pink icing over each of the fondant kisses to define the outline. Leave to set.

COOKIE TIP

These cookies could be presented in a pretty giftbox with tissue paper and ribbons.

STAINED GLASS CHRISTMAS Cookies

These cookies are really easy to make and yet look so impressive. They make great gifts for the festive season.

MAKES: 12
BAKING TIME: 14 MINUTES

INGREDIENTS
175g plain flour
75g butter
3 tablespoons caster sugar
1 egg white
2 tablespoons orange juice
225g hard sweets in assorted colours
Thin ribbon or cord

COOKIE TIP
These cookies look wonderful when hung on the Christmas tree or beside candles, to catch the light.

1. Preheat the oven to 180°C/350°F/Gas mark 4. Line baking sheets with baking paper.
2. Put the flour into a bowl and blend in the butter. Stir in the sugar, egg white and enough orange juice to mix to a soft dough. Knead lightly.
3. Roll out the dough on a lightly floured surface and cut into shapes such as stars, hearts, flowers, Christmas trees etc. Cut out the centres of the cookies using a similar shaped cutter or a plain round cutter.
4. Make a hole on the top of the cookie with a skewer. Place on the prepared baking sheet and bake in the oven for 4 minutes. Remove and place a sweet in the centre of each cookie and return to the oven for a further 10 minutes or until the cookies are golden brown and the sweets have melted and filled the centres of the cookies.
5. Remove from the oven and put a skewer in the holes at the top of each cookies to open them up. Leave the cookies on the baking sheet until cool and set and then peel them off. Thread ribbon or cord through the holes at the top of each cookie.

SNOWFLAKE Cookies

Leave these cookies out for a late-night treat for Santa Claus.

MAKES: 20
BAKING TIME: 6–8 MINUTES

INGREDIENTS
150g plain flour
115g butter
150g icing sugar
½ teaspoon ground cardamom
1 egg yolk
1 tablespoon milk
½ teaspoon vanilla extract
175g white fondant
1 tablespoon sugar
Silver balls for decoration

1. Put the flour, butter and half the icing sugar into a mixing bowl or food processor and mix until it resembles fine breadcrumbs. Add the ground cardamom, egg yolk, milk and vanilla extract and mix until it forms a soft ball. Chill for 30 minutes.

2. Preheat the oven to 200°C/400°F/Gas mark 6. Roll out the dough on a lightly floured surface to 5mm thickness and cut out 20 cookies using a snowflake paper template. Evenly space apart on two baking sheets and bake for 6–8 minutes. Cool on the baking sheets for 10 minutes before transferring to a wire rack to cool completely.

3. Roll out the fondant on a surface lightly dusted with icing sugar to 3mm thickness and cut out 20 snowflakes the same size as the cookies.

4. Mix the remaining icing sugar with 2 teaspoons water to a thick paste, spoon into a paper piping bag and snip off the tip. Pipe small dots over the cookies and lift the fondant snowflakes on top, pressing down lightly to secure. Push the fondant in all around the shape to leave a small gap between the cookie and the fondant. Use the remaining glacé icing to pipe snowflake lines over the fondant icing. Sprinkle immediately with the sugar and decorate with the silver balls.

GINGERBREAD CHRISTMAS Cookies

To be able to hang the cookies make a hole at the top of each one before baking. Reopen the hole as soon as they come out of the oven.

MAKES: 30–40
BAKING TIME: 10–12 MINUTES

INGREDIENTS
350g plain flour
1 tablespoon baking powder
2 teaspoons ground ginger
½ teaspoon ground allspice
50ml black treacle
50ml golden syrup
6 tablespoons butter
3 tablespoons soft dark brown sugar
1 egg, beaten

ICING
155g icing sugar
1 tablespoon lemon juice

1. Lightly grease two baking sheets. Sift the flour, baking powder and spices together into a bowl.

2. Place the treacle, golden syrup, butter and brown sugar in a small saucepan and heat gently, stirring until well combined.

3. Cool slightly, then beat in the egg. Pour into the dry ingredients and mix to form a firm dough. Rest for a few minutes, then knead gently until smooth.

4. Preheat the oven to 180°C/350°F/Gas mark 4. On a lightly floured surface roll out the dough to 5mm thick, and cut out cookies with biscuit cutters. Place on the baking sheets and bake until crisp and golden, 10–12 minutes. Let cool on the baking sheets for 2–3 minutes, then transfer to a wire rack to cool completely.

5. To make the icing, sift the icing sugar into a bowl, add the lemon juice and mix until smooth. Spread or pipe over the cookies. Stand until the icing has set, 1–2 hours. Store in an airtight container for up to two weeks.

SPECULAAS

A traditional Dutch cookie these are eaten in Holland around the feast of St Nicholas, which is 6 December. They are made from a spicy dough wrapped around a soft marzipan filling.

MAKES: **35**
BAKING TIME: **35 MINUTES**

INGREDIENTS
180g hazelnuts, toasted and ground
170g ground almonds
150g caster sugar
170g icing sugar
1 egg, beaten
2–3 teaspoons lemon juice

DOUGH
250g self-raising flour
1 teaspoon mixed spice
75g light brown sugar
115g unsalted butter
2 eggs
1 tablespoon milk
1 tablespoon caster sugar
About 35 blanched almond halves

1. Put all the filling ingredients into a bowl and mix to a firm paste. Divide in half and roll each piece to a sausage shape about 25cm long. Wrap in clingfilm and chill while making the dough.
2. Sift the flour and spice into a bowl and stir in the sugar. Blend in the butter. Beat one of the eggs and add to the mixture and mix together to form a soft, but firm dough. Knead lightly and chill for 15 minutes.
3. Preheat the oven to 180°C/350°F/Gas mark 4. Line a baking sheet with baking paper.
4. Roll out the dough to a 30cm square and cut in half to make two strips. Beat the remaining egg and use to brush all over the pastry strips. Place a roll of filling on each strip and roll up like a sausage roll to completely enclose the filling. Place join side down on the prepared baking sheets.
5. Beat the remains of the egg with the milk and sugar and brush over the rolls. Decorate with halved almonds all along the top. Bake for about 35 minutes until golden brown. Allow to become cold before cutting diagonally into slices.

DEEP FRIED CHRISTMAS Cookies

In Norway these cookies are called reindeer antlers and are made at Christmas, but there are variations all over Europe variously known as 'bits and pieces', 'rags and tatters' and so on. It is best to make the dough the day before and leave in the refrigerator to firm up.

MAKES: 30

INGREDIENTS
2 egg yolks
50g caster sugar
4 tablespoons double cream
1 tablespoon brandy
1 teaspoon ground cardamom
1 teaspoon finely grated lemon rind
50g butter
200g plain flour
Vegetable oil for deep-frying
Sugar and cinnamon for dusting

1. Put the egg yolks and sugar into a bowl and whisk until thick and pale. Add the cream, brandy, cardamom and lemon rind. Blend the butter into the flour. Add the egg mixture to the flour and mix to a soft dough. Cover in clingfilm and leave in the refrigerator overnight.
2. The next day, roll out the dough on a lightly floured surface to 5mm thickness. Using a zigzag pastry wheel cut into strips 5 x 10cm. Cut a slit 2.5cm long lengthways in the centre of each rectangle. Pull one end of the strip through this slit to make a half bow shape.
3. Heat the oil until a cube of bread browns in 1 minute. Deep-fry the cookies a few at a time until golden brown. Remove with a slotted spoon and drain on kitchen towels. Dust liberally with mixed sugar and cinnamon.

RUSSIAN Teacakes

These buttery sugar-dusted teacakes are often served at weddings. When made with pecans they are known as Mexican or Portuguese wedding cakes and when made with almonds they are the Greek version known as kourabiedes.

MAKES: 20
BAKING TIME: 15 MINUTES

INGREDIENTS
115g unsalted butter
2 teaspoons orange flower water
50g icing sugar
90g plain flour
25g lightly toasted ground walnuts
25g lightly toasted walnut pieces, chopped
Icing sugar for dusting

1. Preheat the oven to 180°C/350°F/Gas mark 4. Line baking sheets with baking paper. Beat the butter until soft and creamy.
2. Beat in the orange flower water. Add the icing sugar and beat until fluffy. Add the flour, ground and chopped walnuts and mix well using your hand to bring the mixture together. Don't over work the dough. Chill if the mixture is a little soft.
3. Either roll the mixture into balls or shape pieces of dough into sausages about 7.5cm long. Curve each one into a crescent shape and place well apart on the prepared baking sheets.
4. Bake in the oven for about 15 minutes or until firm and still pale in colour. Cool for about 5 minutes and then dredge liberally with icing sugar.

PERSIAN RICE Cookies

These pretty rose-scented cookies are traditionally offered at special occasions such as weddings.

MAKES: 20
BAKING TIME: 18–20 MINUTES

INGREDIENTS

DOUGH
75g icing sugar
225g very soft unsalted butter
300g rice flour
75g self-raising flour
1 egg yolk
1 tablespoon rose water

TOPPING
150g sifted icing sugar
Rose water
Pink food colouring (optional)
Crystallized rose petals for decoration

1. Put all the ingredients for the dough into a bowl and mix well together. Wrap in clingfilm and chill until firm.

2. Preheat the oven to 180°C/350°F/Gas mark 4. Line baking sheets with baking paper.

3. Shape the mixture into balls the size of large walnuts. Place well apart on the prepared baking sheets and flatten each one slightly.

4. Bake for 18–20 minutes until firm but still pale. Cool completely on the sheets, as these cookies are extremely crumbly while hot.

5. To make the topping put the icing sugar into a bowl and add just enough rose water to mix to a thick flowing consistency. If desired add a touch of pink colouring to make a very pale shade. Drizzle the icing over the cookies and decorate with crystallized rose petals.

COOKIE TIP
To prevent baking paper slipping off baking sheets, sprinkle the sheet with a few drops of water beforehand.

EASTER Bonnets

These pretty, colourful cookies make wonderful easter gifts.

MAKES: 18
BAKING TIME: 10–12 MINUTES

INGREDIENTS

175g butter
175g sugar
1 large egg, beaten
350g plain flour
1 teaspoon baking powder
1 teaspoon vanilla extract
Finely grated rind and juice of 1 small orange
500g white fondant
Red and yellow food colouring
Coloured balls and ribbon for decoration
115g creamed coconut
50g icing sugar

1. Cream the butter and sugar together until pale, beat in the egg and stir in the flour, baking powder, vanilla extract, orange rind and a little of the orange juice to bind to a soft, pliable dough. Chill for 30 minutes.
2. Preheat the oven to 180°C/350°F/Gas mark 4. Roll out on a lightly floured surface to a 5mm thickness and cut out 18 rounds with a 8cm round cutter. Space out the rounds on two baking sheets and bake for 10–12 minutes. Cool on the baking sheets for 10 minutes before transferring to a wire rack to cool completely.
3. Pinch off small balls of fondant and roll out on a surface dusted with icing sugar to an 3mm thickness. Cut out tiny flower shapes to decorate the bonnets and push a coloured ball into the centre of each. Colour half the remaining fondant pink and half yellow and roll out to an 3mm thickness. Cut out nine rounds measuring 8cm from each.
4. Warm the remaining orange juice and mix 2 tablespoons with the creamed coconut and icing sugar to make a smooth paste. Spoon a teaspoonful of the mixture into the centre of each cookie. Cover with the rounds of coloured fondant and press down lightly to shape the bonnet. Decorate with the ribbon and flowers, securing them with a little icing sugar mixed with water.

EASTER Cookies

These currant-filled cookies are traditionally baked for the Christian festival of Easter and in the past they would be eaten after church on Easter morning. They are tied with thin ribbon in bundles of three to represent the Trinity.

MAKES: 18
BAKING TIME: 15–20 MINUTES

INGREDIENTS
180g plain flour
50g rice flour
1 teaspoon mixed spice
115g butter
115g caster sugar
2 egg yolks
50g currants
1 tablespoon chopped mixed peel
1–2 tablespoons milk
1 egg white, very lightly beaten
Caster sugar to sprinkle

1. Preheat the oven to 180°C/350°F/Gas mark 4. Use lightly greased or non-stick baking sheets.
2. Mix together the flour, rice flour and mixed spice. In another bowl cream together the butter and sugar. Beat in the egg yolks and then add the currants and mixed peel. Stir in the flour with enough milk to mix to a fairly stiff dough.
3. Knead lightly and then roll out on a lightly floured surface to 5mm thick. Using a 10cm round fluted cutter cut out cookies and place on the baking sheets.
4. Bake in the oven for 10 minutes then remove from the oven. Brush with the egg white and sprinkle with caster sugar. Return to the oven for a further 5–10 minutes until lightly browned. Place on a wire rack to cool.

MOTHER'S DAY

Handful Of Love

This is a lovely way to say 'thank you' on Mother's Day. Each child can cut out the shape of their hand and decorate with icing and sweets or use purchased icing in tubes and pipe a message on top.

MAKES: 4–6 HANDS DEPENDING ON SIZE
BAKING TIME: 10–15 MINUTES

INGREDIENTS
125g self-raising flour
2 teaspoons ground cinnamon
90g honey
180g soft brown sugar
50g butter
1 egg, beaten
Finely grated rind of 1 lemon
1 tablespoon lemon juice

FOR DECORATION
Blanched almonds
Ready-made icing
Sweets, silver balls etc.

1. Preheat the oven to 180°C/350°F/Gas mark 4. Line a baking sheet with baking paper. Put each child's hand on a piece of thin card (cereal boxes are good) and draw around it. Cut out and use as templates.
2. Put the flour and cinnamon into a bowl and mix together.
3. Put the honey, sugar and butter into a saucepan and heat very gently until melted. Cool slightly. Pour into the flour mixture and add the egg, lemon rind, and juice. Mix to form a soft dough. Knead lightly.
4. Roll out the dough on a lightly floured surface. Using the templates cut out hands from the dough and carefully place on the baking sheet. Re-roll the trimmings and using a small heart-shaped cutter, stamp out a heart for each hand. Place a heart between the first finger and thumb of each hand. Press almonds in the fingers to represent fingernails. Bake in the oven for about 10–15 minutes depending on size.
5. When cold decorate as desired.

CHOCOLATE PUMPKIN Cookies

For this recipe you need a pumpkin-shaped biscuit cutter or draw a pumpkin about 13-15cm in diameter on some card and use as a stencil.

MAKES: ABOUT 8, DEPENDING SIZE OF TEMPLATE
BAKING TIME: 8–10 MINUTES

INGREDIENTS
170g plain flour
85g cocoa powder
1 teaspoon ground cinnamon
170g unsalted butter
170g caster sugar
1 large egg, beaten
300g ready-to-use fondant, coloured orange
1–2 tablespoons honey, warmed

1. Sift together the flour, cocoa and cinnamon. Put the butter and sugar into a bowl and beat until light and fluffy. Beat in the egg. Gradually stir in the flour mixture. Cover in clingfilm and chill until firm.

2. Preheat the oven to 190°C/375°F/Gas mark 5. Line baking sheets with baking paper. On a floured surface roll out the dough to 5mm thick. Using a cutter or the cardboard stencil and a sharp knife, cut out pumpkin shapes.

3. Carefully place on the baking sheets and bake for 8–10 minutes until crisp but not too browned. Leave to cool on a wire rack.

4. Trim the cardboard templates so they are slightly smaller all round. Roll out the fondant, and using the template, cut out one shape for each cookie.

5. Using the back of a knife mark grooves as on a pumpkin. Using a small pointed knife cut out eyes, nose and mouth. Brush each cookie with a little warm honey and place a fondant face on each one. Leave to dry.

HALLOWE'EN TOFFEE APPLE Cookies

Great for those Trick or Treat bags at Hallowe'en these cookies are a mixture of chewy oats, soft apple, sweet raisin, and wonderfully crunchy toffee.

MAKES: 18
BAKING TIME: 12–15 MINUTES

INGREDIENTS
75g plain flour
½ teaspoon bicarbonate of soda
½ teaspoon ground cinnamon
150g unsalted butter
180g soft brown sugar
90g sugar
1 large egg, beaten
250g rolled oats
50g raisins
50g ready-to-eat dried apple rings, roughly chopped
50g chewy toffees, roughly cut up

1. Preheat the oven to 180°C/350°F/Gas mark 4. Line baking sheets with baking paper. Sift together the flour, baking soda, and cinnamon.
2. Put the butter and both sugars into a bowl and beat together until creamy. Add the egg to the butter mixture and beat well. Add the flour mixture and mix thoroughly. Add the oats, raisins, apple and toffee pieces and stir until just combined.
3. Using a small ice cream scoop or large tablespoon place dollops of mixture well apart on to the baking sheets. Bake in the oven for about 12–15 minutes depending on size, or until lightly set in the centre and the edges are just beginning to turn brown,
4. Leave to cool on the sheets for a few minutes and do not touch as the melted toffee will be extremely hot and will set as the mixture cools down. Using a spatula place the cookies on a cooling rack to cool.

SKELETON Lollipops

These crisp, spiced cookies look very impressive. You will need to cut out a template in the shape of a skull to make these cookies.

MAKES: 24
BAKING TIME: 10–12 MINUTES

INGREDIENTS
175g butter
175g sugar
1 egg, beaten
350g plain flour
1 teaspoon baking powder
1 teaspoon mixed spice
Milk
350g white fondant
24 flat wooden lolly sticks
175g plain chocolate
Black food colouring

1. Cream the butter and sugar together until pale, beat in the egg and stir in the flour, baking powder and mixed spice. Stir in a little milk if necessary to bind to a soft, pliable dough. Chill for 30 minutes.
2. Preheat the oven to 180°C/350°F/Gas mark 4. Roll out on a floured surface to 5mm thickness and cut out 24 rounds with a 8cm cutter. Evenly space the rounds apart on two baking sheets, slip a wooden lolly stick 2.5cm under each cookie and press down lightly. Bake for 10–12 minutes. Cool on the baking sheets for 10 minutes before transferring to a wire rack to cool completely.
3. Roll out the fondant on a surface lightly dusted with icing sugar to 3mm thickness. Using a skull paper template, cut out 24 skull shapes, re-rolling the fondant if necessary.
4. Melt the chocolate in a microwave or a glass bowl set over a saucepan of simmering water. Spoon into a paper piping bag and snip off the tip. If necessary, secure the lolly sticks to the cookies with some of the melted chocolate and allow to set. Pipe small dots over the top half of the cookies and arrange the fondant skulls on top. Pipe the eyes and a nose on to each of the skulls, then paint on the mouth and teeth with the black food colouring.

BLUEBERRY SHORTCAKE Cookies

These cookies must be eaten on the day they are made and are especially good warm from the oven. You can substitute with small, halved strawberries or raspberries for a special 4th of July treat.

MAKES: **8**
BAKING TIME: **20 MINUTES**

INGREDIENTS

- 150g plain flour
- 1½ teaspoons baking powder
- 50g unsalted butter
- 50g granulated sugar
- Finely grated rind of 1 lemon
- 120ml soured cream
- 100g fresh blueberries
- Crushed sugar lumps for sprinkling

1. Preheat the oven to 190°C/375°F/Gas mark 5. Line a baking sheet with baking paper.
2. Sift the flour and baking powder into a bowl. Blend in the butter until the mixture resembles fine breadcrumbs. Stir in the sugar and lemon rind.
3. Stir in the soured cream and blueberries and stir until just combined. Spoon 8 mounds, well apart, on the prepared baking sheet. Sprinkle with the crushed sugar lumps and bake in the oven for about 20 minutes until golden and firm in the centre. Serve warm and eat on the day of baking.

COOKIE TIP

Baked and uncooked shaped cookies can be frozen for up to two months. Thaw baked cookies at room temperature and bake uncooked ones from frozen.

RUGELACH

Little crescents made with a delicious cream cheese dough containing a spicy fruit and nut filling. These cookies are traditionally served during the eight-day Jewish festival of Hanukkah.

MAKES: 24–30
BAKING TIME: 15–20 MINUTES

INGREDIENTS

DOUGH

115g unsalted butter, chilled
115g cream cheese
120ml soured cream
250g plain flour

FILLING

50g caster sugar
2 teaspoons ground cinnamon
4 tablespoons raisins, chopped
4 tablespoons ready-to-eat dried apricots, chopped
75g walnuts, finely chopped
Beaten egg for glazing

1. To make the dough put the butter, cream cheese and soured cream into a food processor and blend until just creamy. Add the flour and blend very briefly, using the pulse button until the mixture just comes together. Remove and wrap in clingfilm and chill overnight or at least 6 hours.
2. Preheat the oven to 180°C/350°F/Gas mark 4. Line baking sheets with baking paper. Put the filling ingredients into a bowl and mix together.
3. Divide the dough into four. Take one piece and leave the rest in the refrigerator as it is important to keep the dough as cold as possible as it is very sticky to roll out. Sprinkle a sheet of baking paper with flour, put the dough in the centre and place another sheet of baking paper on top. Quickly roll out the dough to a circle.
4. Cut into six wedges and sprinkle evenly with a quarter of the filling. Starting at the wide end, roll each triangle up towards the point. Curve each roll into a crescent and place with the pointed side down on the baking sheets. Repeat with the remaining dough.
5. Brush with beaten egg and bake in the oven for about 15–20 minutes or until golden brown. Cool on a wire rack.

CHINESE FORTUNE Cookies

The messages in these cookies traditionally contain predictions of the future and are popular at the New Year.

MAKES: 35
BAKING TIME: 5 MINUTES

INGREDIENTS
2 egg whites
50g icing sugar, sifted
1 teaspoon almond extract
2 tablespoons unsalted butter, melted
50g plain flour
25g dessicated coconut, lightly toasted
Icing sugar for sprinkling
Tiny strips of paper with good luck and other appropriate messages typed on them

1. Preheat the oven to 190°C/375°F/Gas mark 5. Prepare two or three sheets of baking paper (they can be used more than once) by cutting them to the size of the baking sheet. Draw two or three rounds of about 7.5cm diameter on each sheet of paper. Place on the baking sheet.

2. Put the egg whites into a bowl and beat until soft peaks form. Beat in the icing sugar a little at a time. Beat in the almond extract and butter. Stir in the flour and mix until smooth.

3. Place a teaspoonful of mixture in the centre of a marked round and spread out thinly and evenly to fit the circle. Sprinkle with a little coconut. Bake one sheet at a time, in the oven, for about 5 minutes or until very lightly brown on the edges.

4. Remove from the oven and immediately lift the cookies from the sheet and loosely fold in half tucking a message inside. Rest the cookie over the rim of a glass so the cookie bends in the centre. Cool and when firm remove to a wire rack. Continue to bake and shape the remaining cookies in the same way. Sprinkle very lightly with icing sugar.

POLENTA & CRANBERRY Cookies

These little cookies are not overly sweet and have a lovely hint of orange and the delightful addition of cranberry. They make an ideal accompaniment to mid-morning or after-dinner coffee.

MAKES: 16
BAKING TIME: 8–10 MINUTES

INGREDIENTS
80g butter
100g fine polenta, plus extra for dusting
115g plain flour
50g caster sugar
1 egg
Finely grated rind of 1 orange
100g dried sweetened cranberries

1. Preheat the oven to 190°C/375°F/Gas mark 5.

2. Put the butter, polenta, and flour into a bowl. Blend in the butter. Stir in the sugar.

3. Add the egg, orange rind, and cranberries and mix well together with your hands until the mixture just comes together.

4. Shape into small sticks and roll in polenta. Place on non-stick baking sheets and bake in the oven for about 8–10 minutes until just beginning to brown.

COOKIE TIP
Only grease baking sheets when a recipe instructs you to. Otherwise the cookies may spread too much and become flat.

GRANDMA'S FAVOURITES

MAPLE GLAZED Cookies

These sticky cookies have a soft, chewy texture that children love.

MAKES: 18
BAKING TIME: 15 MINUTES

INGREDIENTS
175g plain flour
1 teaspoon baking powder
½ teaspoon bicarbonate of soda
6 tablespoons, cut into cubes
75g sugar
50g pecan nuts, chopped
1 egg, lightly beaten
6 tablespoons maple syrup

1. Preheat the oven to 180°C/350°F/Gas mark 4. Lightly grease two baking sheets.

2. Sift the flour, baking powder and bicarbonate of soda into a bowl. Add the butter and blend with your fingertips until the mixture resembles fine breadcrumbs. Stir in the sugar and pecans.

3. Add the egg and 4 tablespoons of the maple syrup and mix until well combined.

4. Drop small heaped tablespoonfuls of the dough, slightly spaced apart on to the baking sheets. Bake until golden, about 15 minutes.

5. Brush the cookies with the remaining maple syrup while still hot, then transfer to a wire rack to cool completely.

COOKIE TIP
Always pay special attention when measuring flour for baking recipes – too much and your cookies will be too hard and too little and they will turn out too flat.

SOURED CREAM & RAISIN Cookies

If your raisins are a bit dried out, plump them up by soaking in hot water for about 10 minutes. Rinse with cool water, squeeze dry and coat lightly in flour from the recipe before adding to the dough.

MAKES: 18
BAKING TIME: 10–12 MINUTES

INGREDIENTS
125g butter
150g sugar
6 tablespoons soured cream
175g plain flour
1 teaspoon bicarbonate of soda
75g raisins

1. Preheat the oven to 180°C/350°F/Gas mark 4. Lightly grease two baking sheets.
2. Cream the butter and sugar together until pale and fluffy. Beat in the soured cream.
3. Sift the flour and bicarbonate of soda together, then beat into the mixture. Stir in the raisins.
4. Drop tablespoons of the dough well apart on the baking sheets. Bake until golden, 10–12 minutes. Cool on the baking sheets for 2–3 minutes, then transfer to a wire rack to cool completely.

COOKIE TIP
Always allow cookies to cool completely before transferring to an airtight storage container.

SPICED BLACK TREACLE Cookies

Rich and spicy, these cookies are delicious served with a cup of coffee.

MAKES: 10–12
BAKING TIME: 12–15 MINUTES

INGREDIENTS
225g sifted plain flour
2 teaspoons bicarbonate of soda
¼ teaspoon salt
¾ teaspoon ground ginger
1 teaspoon ground cinnamon
½ teaspoon ground cloves
1 teaspoon pure vanilla extract
275g butter, softened
200g soft dark brown sugar
1 egg
90g black treacle

1. Preheat the oven to 180°C/350°F/Gas mark 4. Grease two baking sheets.

2. In a large bowl and using an electric mixer, combine the flour, bicarbonate of soda, salt, ginger, cinnamon and cloves. Gradually add the vanilla, butter, sugar, egg and treacle, increasing the speed to medium. Beat for 2 minutes, scraping down the sides of the bowl as necessary.

3. Drop large tablespoonfuls of the dough well apart on to the baking sheets. Bake until the tops are dry, 12–15 minutes. Cool completely on wire racks.

COOKIE TIP

To prevent treacle from clinging to the side of the measuring cup, lightly grease the cup first or spray it with non-stick cooking spray.

OATMEAL RAISIN Cookies

These classic American cookies have stood the test of time. Be sure not to overcook them so that they stay nice and chewy.

MAKES: 10–12
BAKING TIME: 10 MINUTES

INGREDIENTS
150g plain flour
150g rolled oats
1 teaspoon ground ginger
½ teaspoon baking powder
½ teaspoon bicarbonate of soda
150g soft light brown sugar
50g raisins
1 egg, lightly beaten
125ml vegetable oil
4 tablespoons milk

1. Preheat the oven to 200°C/400°F/Gas mark 6. Lightly grease a baking sheet. Mix together the flour, oats, ginger, baking powder, bicarbonate of soda, sugar and raisins in a large bowl.
2. In another bowl, mix together the egg, oil and milk. Make a well in the centre of the dry ingredients and pour in the egg mixture. Mix together well to make a soft dough.
3. Place spoonfuls of the dough well apart on to the baking sheet and flatten slightly with the tines of a fork. Bake until golden, about 10 minutes. Transfer the cookies to a wire rack to cool completely.

APPLE & CRANBERRY Shortcake

These delicious fruity wedges of shortcake are great served as a dessert accompanied by a spoonful of soured cream.

1. Lightly grease a 23cm round loose-based tin.

2. To make the filling, peel, core and slice the apples. Cook gently with 1 tablespoon water for about 5 minutes until the fruit is soft. Stir in the cranberry sauce and allow to cool.

3. Beat the butter and sugar together until light and fluffy. Beat in the egg and vanilla extract. Sift the flour and cornflour together and beat in to form a soft dough.

4. Divide the dough in half and roll out one piece to fit the base of the prepared tin. Prick all over with a fork. Spread the fruit mixture over the dough, leaving a small border around the edge. Dampen the edges with a little water. Roll out the remaining dough and lightly press over the top. Chill for 30 minutes in the refrigerator or 10 minutes in the freezer.

5. Preheat the oven to 180°C/350°F/Gas mark 5. Bake in the centre of the oven for 35–40 minutes until golden. Allow to cool in the tin. When cold, carefully remove from the tin and cut into wedges. Store in a cool place for up to three days.

MAKES: **12**
BAKING TIME: **35–40 MINUTES**

INGREDIENTS

175g butter, softened
75g sugar
1 egg
1 teaspoon. vanilla extract
225g self-raising flour
50g cornflour

FILLING

2 green dessert apples
100g cranberry sauce

BLUEBERRY THUMBPRINT Cookies

The simple, mellow vanilla flavour of these cookies works incredibly well with the tartness of the blueberry jam. For a really traditional American taste, try filling the thumbprint well with peanut butter and jam.

MAKES: 36
BAKING TIME: 10 MINUTES

INGREDIENTS
225g butter, softened
100g icing sugar
1 teaspoon vanilla extract
100g ground almonds
200g plain flour
Blueberry jam
Icing sugar for dusting

1. Lightly grease two baking sheets. Cream the butter and sugar together until pale and fluffy, then beat in the vanilla. Blend in the ground almonds and then gradually add the flour, bringing the mixture together with your hands to form a soft dough as you add the last of the flour.

2. Lightly dust your hands with flour and roll the dough into small balls about the size of a walnut. Arrange on the baking sheets and using your thumb, make a deep hole in the centre of each cookie. Chill for 30 minutes.

3. Preheat the oven to 180°C/350°F/Gas mark 4. Bake the cookies for 10 minutes, then fill each hole with a little jam and return to the oven until pale golden, about 5 minutes. Cool on the baking sheets for a few minutes before transferring to a wire rack to cool completely. Dust with icing sugar to finish.

OATY APPLE Crunchies

A special favourite with kids and adults, the crunchiness of the oats and moistness of the apple sauce gives these cookies great appeal.

MAKES: 18
BAKING TIME: 10–15 MINUTES

INGREDIENTS
175g rolled oats
50g plain flour
150g soft light brown sugar
100g chunky apple sauce
100ml corn oil
1 egg

1. Preheat the oven to 180°C/350°F/Gas mark 4. Lightly grease two baking sheets.
2. Place all the ingredients in a large mixing bowl and beat until well combined.
3. Drop rounded tablespoons of the dough on to the baking sheets. Flatten slightly with the back of a spoon.
4. Bake until golden, 10–15 minutes. Cool on the baking sheets for a few minutes then transfer to a wire rack to cool completely.

COOKIE TIP
If you are cooking with children make sure you clear a large area to work in – a small confined area may cause unnecessary accidents to happen.

MELTING Moments

These pretty cookies take their name from their fabulous melt-in-the-mouth dough.

MAKES: 20
BAKING TIME: 15–20 MINUTES

INGREDIENTS
175g butter, softened
50g sugar
1 egg yolk
175g plain flour
Grated rind of ½ orange or lemon
1 tablespoon orange or lemon juice
Mixed peel for decoration
Icing sugar for dusting

1. Preheat the oven to 190°C/375°F/Gas mark 5. Lightly grease two baking sheets.

2. Cream the butter and sugar together until light and fluffy. Beat in the egg yolk. Work in the flour and orange or lemon rind and juice to form a smooth, thick paste.

3. Spoon the paste into a piping bag fitted with a large star nozzle and pipe rosettes measuring about 5cm across on to the baking sheets. Lightly press some mixed peel into each cookie.

4. Bake until pale golden, 15–20 minutes. Cool on the baking sheets for a few minutes before transferring to a wire rack to cool completely. Dust each cookie with icing sugar.

COOKIE TIP

Only store one kind of cookie in a container. If you mix crisp and soft cookies they will all go soft and end up tasting the same.

STRAWBERRY JAM Delights

Children will love helping to stamp out the rounds and rings in these attractive cookies.

MAKES: 12–16
BAKING TIME: 15 MINUTES

INGREDIENTS
125g butter, softened
50g sugar
1 egg
½ teaspoon vanilla extract
200g plain flour
6 tablespoons cornflour
½ teaspoon baking powder

FILLING
Strawberry or raspberry jam

1. Cream the butter and sugar together until light and fluffy. Beat in the egg and vanilla. Sift the flour, cornflour and baking powder together and beat in to form a soft dough.

2. Preheat the oven to 180°C/350°F/Gas mark 4. Lightly grease two baking sheets.

3. Roll out the dough on a lightly floured surface to about 3mm thick and cut into rounds using a 6cm biscuit cutter. Cut a 2.5cm circle from the centre of half the rounds. The trimmings can be re-rolled and used to make additional cookies. Make sure you have an equal number of rounds and rings. Arrange on the baking sheets.

4. Bake until pale golden, about 15 minutes. Cool on the baking sheets for a few minutes before transferring to a wire rack to cool completely.

5. When cooled completely, spread the rounds with the jam and place a ring on top, pushing lightly together. Store in an airtight container for up to one week.

SPICY CRANBERRY Cookies

Dried cranberries can be bought sweetened or unsweetened. Sweetened berries resemble red raisins; unsweetened cranberries taste slightly tart.

MAKES: 15
BAKING TIME: 15–18 MINUTES

INGREDIENTS
125g butter, softened
100g sugar
1 egg, separated
50g dried cranberries
175g plain flour
½ teaspoon mixed spice
Demerara sugar for sprinkling

1. Preheat the oven to 180°C/350°F/Gas mark 4. Lightly grease two baking sheets. Cream the butter and sugar together until light and fluffy, then beat in the egg yolk. Stir in the cranberries.

2. Sift together the flour and spice. Add to the bowl and mix to form a stiff dough. Roll out the dough on a lightly floured surface to about 3mm thick and cut into 7.5cm rounds.

3. Arrange on the baking sheets. Lightly beat the egg white and brush over the surface of each circle. Sprinkle with the demerara sugar.

4. Bake until golden and brown, 15–18 minutes. Cool for a few minutes on the baking sheets, then transfer to a wire rack to cool completely. Store in an airtight container for up to one week.

COOKIE TIP

If you have difficulty separating egg yolks from whites, tap the shell sharply and break the egg on to a saucer. Place an egg cup upside down over the yolk and tip the saucer so the white slides into the bowl.

OAT CRUNCH Cookies

While the cookies are hot, press an indentation into the centre of each one with your thumb and fill with a little jam.

MAKES: 20
BAKING TIME: 16–18 MINUTES

INGREDIENTS
150g plain flour
1 teaspoon bicarbonate of soda
175g rolled oats
125g butter
100g soft light brown sugar
1 tablespoon golden syrup
1 tablespoon water

1. Preheat the oven to 180°C/350°F/Gas mark 4. Lightly grease two baking sheets. Sift the flour and bicarbonate of soda into a mixing bowl. Stir in the oats.

2. Place the butter, sugar, golden syrup, and 1 tablespoon water in a saucepan and heat gently, stirring until combined. Add to the dry ingredients and stir until well mixed.

3. Take small amounts of the dough, each about the size of a walnut, and roll into balls. Space them well apart on the baking sheets and flatten slightly.

4. Bake until golden, 16–18 minutes. Cool on the baking sheets for 2–3 minutes, then transfer to a wire rack to cool completely. Store in an airtight container for up to five days.

COOKIE TIP
Cool cookies on wire racks without touching each other to keep them from sticking together.

ALMOND Macaroons

Macaroons are traditionally made on edible rice paper, but if you have trouble finding it, then dust the baking sheets liberally with semolina and flour.

MAKES: 12
BAKING TIME: 15–20 MINUTES

INGREDIENTS
- 100g ground almonds
- 175g caster sugar
- 2 tablespoons semolina or ground rice
- 2 egg whites
- Few drops of almond extract
- 100g plain chocolate chips
- Whole blanched almonds for decoration

1. Preheat the oven to 160°C/325°F/Gas mark 4. Line two baking sheets with rice paper.

2. Mix the almonds, sugar and semolina. In a separate bowl, beat the egg whites until stiff. Add the almond extract.

3. Gradually fold in the sugar and almond mixture until quite stiff.

4. Fold in the chocolate chips. Place tablespoonful of mixture on to the baking sheets, well spaced out. Place an almond on top of each and bake until golden, 15–20 minutes. Cool, then tear the rice paper between each biscuit, or use a wire rack if you're not using paper.

COOKIE TIP
Baked and uncooked shaped cookies can be frozen for up to two months. Thaw baked cookies at room temperature and bake uncooked ones from frozen.

HONEY Cookies

Orange and walnut flavoured cookies dipped in honey for a real old-fashioned taste.

MAKES: 30
BAKING TIME: 15–20 MINUTES

INGREDIENTS
125g butter
Finely grated rind of 1 orange
80g caster sugar
80ml sunflower oil
300g plain flour
150g self-raising flour
25g finely chopped walnuts
160ml orange juice
250ml honey
2 tablespoons finely chopped walnuts for sprinkling

1. Preheat the oven to 180°C/350°F/Gas mark 4. Put the butter, orange rind and sugar into a bowl and beat well together. Gradually beat in the oil until the mixture is light and fluffy.

2. Stir in the flours, nuts and juice and mix to a soft dough.

3. Using two tablespoons shape the mixture into ovals and place on baking sheets lined with baking paper. Bake in the oven for 15–20 minutes until lightly browned.

4. Heat the honey in a small saucepan. Making sure the honey is not too hot, dip the warm cookies in the honey to coat. Place on a wire rack over a tray. Sprinkle with the chopped nuts.

COOKIE TIP
Make sure the honey glaze has set completely before transferring the cookies to a storage container.

DUTCH Shortcakes

Crisp buttery shortcakes baked in strips and then cut up.

MAKES: 18
BAKING TIME: 15–20 MINUTES

INGREDIENTS
2 tablespoons custard powder (or cornflour)
180g plain flour
150g butter
80g caster sugar
1 egg yolk

1. Preheat the oven to 180°C/350°F/Gas mark 4. Sift the custard powder and flour together.

2. Cream the butter and sugar together and beat in the egg yolk. Mix in the flour well.

3. Put the mixture into a piping bag fitted with a large star nozzle and pipe three flat zigzag lines about 5 x 25cm on a non-stick baking sheet.

4. Bake in the oven for 15–20 minutes until pale golden brown. While still warm cut each piece into six and cool on a wire rack.

COOKIE TIP

If you are looking out for your health you may be considering replacing the butter with low fat margarine, but be aware that reducing the sugar and fat in the ingredients can make cookies more cake-like.

FIG & DATE Rolls

Short crumbly pastry filled with moist dates and figs. These cookies keep well in an airtight container.

MAKES: 24
BAKING TIME: 20–25 MINUTES

INGREDIENTS

FILLING
300g dried figs, finely chopped
80g stoned dates, finely chopped
125ml water
Finely grated rind of 1 lemon
100g caster sugar

DOUGH
125g butter
75g caster sugar
1 teaspoon ground cinnamon
1 egg
75g ground almonds
225g plain flour

1. To make the filling put all the ingredients into a saucepan and stir over a gentle heat until the sugar is dissolved. Simmer uncovered for about 15 minutes until the mixture is thick and pulpy. Cool.

2. To make the dough beat together the butter, sugar, cinnamon and egg. Stir in the ground almonds and flour. Knead lightly and divide into four. Wrap each portion in clingfilm and chill for 30 minutes.

3. Preheat the oven to 180°C/350°F/Gas mark 4. Roll out each portion of dough between sheets of baking paper to 10 x 20cm. Spread a quarter of the filling along each rectangle leaving a 1cm border. Fold the long sides over the filling to meet in the centre and press gently together. Tuck the ends under.

4. Place the rolls seam-side down, on non-stick baking sheets. Bake for 20–25 minutes until lightly browned. Remove and leave to cool.

5. When cold cut into slices.

CARDAMOM GINGER Crisps

Ideal for dunking these crisp little fingers have the unusual addition of ground cardamom.

MAKES: 50
BAKING TIME: 10–15 MINUTES

INGREDIENTS
125g butter
125g soft light brown sugar
1 teaspoon ground cardamom
½ teaspoon ground cinnamon
Pinch of ground nutmeg
2 egg yolks
180g plain flour
2 tablespoons crystallized ginger, finely chopped

1. Put the butter, sugar, spices and egg yolks into a bowl and beat well together.

2. Stir in the flour and crystallized ginger. Knead until smooth. Shape into a block about 7.5 x 28cm. Wrap in baking paper and chill until firm.

3. Preheat the oven to 160°C/325°F/Gas mark 3. Cut the dough into 3mm slices and place on baking sheets lined with baking paper. Bake in the oven for 10–15 minutes until golden. Cool on a wire rack.

COOKIE TIP

Always stir flour prior to measuring. Flour settles as it sits and if you do not stir it you may end up adding too much to your cookies.

APPLE STREUSEL Bars

These fruity, crunchy bars make a wonderful afternoon snack with a cup of tea.

MAKES: 12–14
BAKING TIME: 45 MINUTES

INGREDIENTS
225g self-raising flour
50g ground almonds
175g butter
75g soft light brown sugar
2 egg yolks

TOPPING
3 dessert apples
50g sultanas (optional)
175g plain flour
½ teaspoon ground cloves
75g butter
75g soft brown sugar

1. Preheat the oven to 180°C/350°F/Gas mark 4. Lightly grease a 20 x 28cm oblong baking tin.

2. Sift the self-raising flour into a mixing bowl and stir in the almonds. Cut the butter into cubes and blend into the mixture until it resembles breadcrumbs. Stir in the brown sugar. Add the egg yolks and work the mixture together to form a firm dough. Press out to line the base of the prepared tin. Prick all over and chill while making the topping.

3. To make the topping, peel, core and roughly chop the apples, then place in a saucepan with 2 tablespoons water. Cook gently for about 3–4 minutes until tender. Stir in the sultanas if using.

4. Sift the flour and cloves into another bowl. Blend in the butter until the mixture resembles crumbs. Stir in the brown sugar. Spread the apple mixture over the dough and sprinkle the streusel mixture on top. Bake for about 45 minutes until the topping is golden.

5. Cool in the tin and serve cut into bars or squares. Store in the refrigerator for up to four days.

LAVENDER SCENTED Shortbread

A popular remedy in traditional medicine, lavender is said to help promote sleep. Try one of these fragrant shortbreads before going to bed and they should really do the trick.

MAKES: 18–20
BAKING TIME: 15–20 MINUTES

INGREDIENTS
125g caster sugar
4 dried lavender flowers, natural and unsprayed
225g butter
225g plain flour
120g ground rice
Pinch of salt
Extra lavender flowers and caster sugar for decoration

1. Line two baking sheets with greaseproof paper.
2. Put the sugar and lavender in a food processor and whiz for about 10 seconds.
3. Cream together the butter and sugar until light and fluffy, then stir in the flour, ground rice and salt until the mixture resembles breadcrumbs.
4. Using your hands, gather the dough together and knead until it forms a ball. Roll into a sausage shape and then shape into a long block about 5cm thick. Wrap in clingfilm and chill for about 30 minutes or until firm.
5. Preheat the oven to 190°C/375°F/Gas mark 5. Slice the dough into 5mm squares and place on the baking sheets. Bake for 15–20 minutes or until pale golden. Sprinkle with sugar and leave on the baking sheets for 10 minutes, then transfer to a wire rack to cool completely.

GOURMET COOKIES

WHITE CHOCOLATE & NUT Cookies

If you prefer, substitute the macadamias for another variety of nut.

MAKES: 12–15
BAKING TIME: 15–18 MINUTES

INGREDIENTS
255g plain flour
1 teaspoon bicarbonate of soda
30g plain cocoa powder
½ teaspoon salt
225g unsalted butter, softened
225g soft light brown sugar, firmly packed
100g sugar
2 large eggs
2 teaspoons vanilla extract
230g white chocolate chips
230g macadamia nuts, roughly chopped

1. Preheat the oven to 190°C/375°F/Gas mark 5. Lightly grease two baking sheets.

2. In a medium bowl, sift together the flour, bicarbonate of soda, cocoa powder and salt. Set aside.

3. Cream the butter and sugars together until light and fluffy. Beat in the eggs and vanilla. Gently stir in the flour mixture until just combined. Fold in the white chocolate and macadamia nuts.

4. Drop large rounded tablespoons of the dough on to the baking sheets, well spaced apart as the cookies will spread. Bake until firm, 15–18 minutes. Cool on the baking sheets for a few minutes before transferring to a wire rack to cool completely.

COOKIE TIP
Pack even more of a chocolate punch by adding some plain chocolate chips.

ORANGE PECAN Cookies

These cookies will keep in an airtight container – if you can resist eating them all at once.

MAKES: 24
BAKING TIME: 10–12 MINUTES

INGREDIENTS
6 tablespoons butter
6 tablespoons sugar
6 tablespoons soft light brown sugar
1 egg
Grated rind of 1 orange
2 tablespoons orange juice
175g plain flour
½ teaspoon bicarbonate of soda
85g pecan nuts, roughly chopped

1. Preheat the oven to 180°C/350°F/Gas mark 4. Lightly grease two baking sheets.

2. Cream the butter and sugars together until pale and fluffy. Beat in the egg, orange rind and juice.

3. Sift the flour and baking soda together and beat into the mixture. Stir in the nuts.

4. Drop tablespoons of the dough well apart on to the baking sheets. Bake until golden, 10–12 minutes. Leave the cookies to cool on the baking sheets for 2–3 minutes, then transfer to a wire rack to cool completely. Store in an airtight container for up to five days.

COOKIE TIP
Add a few of the chopped nuts to the top of the cookies before baking to give an extra crunch.

PINEAPPLE Macaroons

Enjoy these soft, fruity macaroons with mid-morning coffee or afternoon tea.

MAKES: 20–24
BAKING TIME: 25–30 MINUTES

INGREDIENTS
400g canned pineapple rings in natural juice
10–12 glacé cherries
3 egg whites
200g sugar
200g flaked coconut

COOKIE TIP
Vary the flavouring in these chewy cookies or leave out the pineapple if you prefer a traditional macaroon.

1. Preheat the oven to 160°C/325°F/Gas mark 3. Line two baking sheets with non-stick baking paper.
2. Drain the pineapple well and chop finely. Place in a sieve and squeeze out as much juice as possible. Halve the cherries.
3. Beat the egg whites to stiff peaks. Gradually beat in the sugar. Fold in the pineapple and coconut until well combined.
4. Drop spoonfuls of the dough on to the lined baking sheets, piling into a pyramid shape. Allow space for the cookies to spread slightly. Top each with half a cherry.
5. Bake until lightly browned and crisp, 25–30 minutes. Cool on the baking sheets, then carefully remove and store in an airtight container for up to three days. Do not freeze.

SPICED PUMPKIN & PECAN Crisps

These slightly spiced cookies are a great light snack.

MAKES: 24–30
BAKING TIME: 25–30 MINUTES

INGREDIENTS
125g butter, softened
150g plain flour
150g soft light brown sugar
150g tinned pumpkin or cooked and mashed pumpkin
1 egg
2 teaspoons ground cinnamon
½ teaspoon vanilla extract
½ teaspoon baking powder
1 teaspoon bicarbonate of soda
½ teaspoon ground nutmeg
75g wholemeal flour
75g pecan nuts, roughly chopped
150g raisins

ICING
4 tablespoons unsalted butter
150g icing sugar
1½ teaspoons vanilla extract
2 tablespoons milk

1. Preheat the oven to 190°C/375°F/Gas mark 5. Lightly grease two baking sheets.

2. Using an electric beater, beat the butter until fluffy. Add the flour, sugar, pumpkin, egg, cinnamon, vanilla, baking powder, bicarbonate of soda and nutmeg. Beat until well combined, scraping down the sides of the bowl. Add the wholemeal flour, nuts and raisins and fold in until just combined.

3. Drop the dough in large tablespoonfuls, well spaced apart on to the baking sheets. Bake until golden, 25–30 minutes. Remove from the oven and cool on a wire rack.

4. To make the icing, melt the butter over a medium heat in a small pan and continue cooking until light golden brown. Remove from the heat and add the icing sugar, vanilla and milk. Mix until smooth, adding a little more milk or icing sugar as necessary to make the mixture spreadable. Cool until thick, then spread generously over the cooled cookies.

DARK CHOCOLATE & PECAN Brownies

Have a batch of these rich, sticky brownies ready for a midnight treat – served with a big scoop of ice cream.

MAKES: 12
BAKING TIME: 20–25 MINUTES

INGREDIENTS
115g plain chocolate
175g butter
450g granulated sugar
3 eggs
200g plain flour
1½ teaspoons vanilla extract
125g pecan nuts

1. Preheat the oven to 180°C/350°F/Gas mark 4. Grease a 33 x 23cm non-stick baking tin. Break the plain chocolate into pieces and place in a saucepan with the butter. Melt over a gentle heat, stirring occasionally, and then take the pan off the heat.

2. Add the sugar to the chocolate and stir until dissolved. Beat in the eggs, and then stir in the flour, vanilla extract and pecan nuts. Pour the mixture into the saucepan and level the surface.

3. Bake for 20–25 minutes or until the top of the brownies are shiny and set. Place the tin of brownies on a wire rack to cool, then cut into squares and serve.

COOKIE TIP

If you can keep your hands off them for long enough, these cookies will keep for several days in an airtight container.

WALNUT Kisses

When grinding walnuts for these cookies, use on and off pulses of the food processor to prevent them from turning to paste.

MAKES: 40
BAKING TIME: 30 MINUTES

INGREDIENTS
50g walnuts
100g icing sugar
2 egg whites

COOKIE TIP
Almonds work just as well as walnuts in this recipe.

1. Preheat the oven to 150°C/300°F/Gas mark 2. Line two baking sheets with non-stick baking paper.
2. Grind the walnuts in a food processor until very finely chopped. Sift the icing sugar into a bowl.
3. Put the egg white in a large, grease-free mixing bowl and beat until frothy. Gradually add the icing sugar and beat until combined.
4. Place the bowl over a saucepan of gently simmering water and beat until the mixture is very thick and stands in stiff peaks. Remove from the saucepan and beat until cold.
5. Carefully fold in the ground walnuts until just blended, then spoon into a piping bag fitted with a large plain or star nozzle. Pipe small rosettes or balls slightly spaced on to the baking sheets.
6. Bake until the cookies can be easily removed from the paper, about 30 minutes. Cool and store in an airtight container.

ICED COFFEE Creams

Simple to make with a sophisticated flavour, these iced cookies are delicious with morning coffee.

MAKES: 20
BAKING TIME: 15 MINUTES

INGREDIENTS
125g butter, softened
100g sugar
50ml strong black coffee
250g plain flour
3 tablespoons cornflour

FILLING
4 tablespoons butter, softened
175g icing sugar
2 tablespoons strong black coffee

ICING
75g icing sugar
1–2 teaspoons strong black coffee

1. Preheat the oven to 180°C/350°F/Gas mark 4. Lightly grease two baking sheets.

2. Cream the butter and sugar together until light and fluffy. Beat in the remaining ingredients, bringing the mixture together to form a firm dough.

3. Roll out the dough on a lightly floured surface to about 3mm thick and cut out with biscuit cutter shapes of your choice. Arrange on baking sheets.

4. Bake until lightly browned, about 15 minutes. Cool on the baking sheets for a few minutes before transferring to a wire rack to cool completely.

5. To make the filling, cream the butter until fluffy, then gradually beat in the icing sugar and coffee. Sandwich the cookies together in pairs with the filling.

6. To make the icing, sift the icing sugar into a bowl and stir in enough coffee to form a smooth icing. Spread over the tops of the cookies and let set.

LACE Cookies

You can make these cookies slightly larger than usual as they look lovely piled up and served with ice cream or elegant cream desserts.

MAKES: 12–14
BAKING TIME: 5–7 MINUTES

INGREDIENTS
75g butter
75g rolled oats
115g icing sugar
1 egg, beaten
2 teaspoons plain flour
1 teaspoon bicarbonate of soda
½ teaspoon ground cinnamon

1. Preheat the oven to 180°C/350°F/Gas mark 4. Line baking sheets with baking paper. Melt the butter in a saucepan and remove from the heat. Stir in all the remaining ingredients.

2. Put 3–4 heaped teaspoonfuls of the mixture on to the prepared baking sheets.

3. Bake in the oven for about 5–7 minutes or until dark golden brown.

4. Leave to cool for a few minutes on the baking sheets and then carefully remove to a wire rack using a large spatula.

COOKIE TIP

Don't be tempted to put more than three or four of these cookies on the baking sheet and make sure they are spaced well apart.

PISTACHIO Biscotti

Decorate these cookies by drizzling a little chocolate over the top.

MAKES: 50
BAKING TIME: 40 MINUTES

INGREDIENTS
175g pistachios
460g plain flour
125g coarse polenta
2 teaspoons baking powder
125g butter
100g sugar
3 eggs
1 teaspoon grated lemon rind
1 teaspoon grated orange rind
2 tablespoons orange juice
½ teaspoon almond extract
1 teaspoon fennel seeds, crushed (optional)

1. Preheat the oven to 180°C/350°F/Gas mark 4. Lightly grease two baking sheets.
2. Roughly chop half the pistachios. Sift the flour, polenta, and baking powder together.
3. Cream the butter and sugar together until pale and fluffy. Beat in the eggs one at a time. Beat in the lemon and orange rind, juice, almond extract and fennel seeds. Do not worry if the mixture looks curdled at this stage, as this is normal.
4. Beat in the chopped and whole pistachios. Finally, work in the flour mixture, using your hands to mix it to a soft dough. Divide the dough into four pieces and roll each piece into a log shape about 30cm long on a lightly floured surface. Place on the baking sheets and flatten slightly.
5. Bake until the logs are risen and golden, about 30 minutes; reverse the baking sheets halfway through the baking time. Remove from the oven and cool slightly.
6. Reduce the oven temperature to 160°C/325°F/Gas mark 3. When the logs are cool enough to handle, cut each one diagonally into 1cm slices. Arrange cut-side down on the baking sheets and return to the oven until crisp and golden, about 10 minutes. Store in an airtight container for up to two weeks.

LIME MUSCOVADO SUGAR Cookies

The lime icing lends a real tang to these sophisticated cookies.

MAKES: 22
BAKING TIME: 10–12 MINUTES

INGREDIENTS
125g butter
100g soft muscovado sugar
1 egg, beaten
Grated rind of 1 lime
1 tablespoon lime juice
300g plain flour
1 teaspoon bicarbonate of soda

ICING
160g icing sugar
1–2 tablespoons fresh lime juice
Grated zest of 1 lime

1. Preheat the oven to 180°C/350°F/Gas mark 4. Lightly grease two baking sheets. Cream the butter and brown sugar together until fluffy. Beat in the egg, lime rind, and juice.

2. Sift together the flour and bicarbonate of soda, then beat into the butter mixture. Work together with your hands to form a soft dough.

3. On a lightly floured surface, roll out the dough to 5mm thick and cut out cookies with biscuit cutters. Place on the baking sheets and bake until crisp and golden, 10–12 minutes. Cool on the baking sheets for 2–3 minutes, then transfer to a wire rack to cool completely.

4. To make the icing, sift the icing sugar into a bowl and mix in the lime juice and zest until smooth. Spread or pipe over the cookies. Dry for 1–2 hours or until the icing has set. Store in an airtight container for up to five days.

CHEESECAKE SWIRL Brownies

These are irresistible – a chocolate brownie base topped with brownie mixture and cream cheese. Cut into small squares to serve as they are rather rich but perfectly heavenly and make a great dessert when served with fresh raspberries.

MAKES: 16
BAKING TIME: 30 MINUTES

INGREDIENTS

CHEESECAKE MIX
1 egg
225g full-fat cream cheese
50g caster sugar
1 teaspoon vanilla extract

BROWNIE MIX
115g plain chocolate
115g unsalted butter
150g soft light brown sugar
2 eggs, beaten
50g plain flour

1. Preheat the oven to 160°C/325°F/Gas mark 3. Grease and base line a 20cm square shallow cake pan.
2. To make the cheesecake mixture, put all the ingredients into a bowl and beat well together.
3. To make the brownie mixture, melt the chocolate and butter together in a bowl in the microwave or over a saucepan of hot water. When melted, remove from the heat, stir well and stir in the sugar. Add the eggs a little at a time and beat well. Gently fold in the flour.
4. Spread two-thirds of the brownie mixture in the base of the prepared tin. Spread the cheesecake mixture on top. Spoon the remaining brownie mixture on top in heaps. Using a skewer, swirl the mixtures together.
5. Bake in the oven for about 30 minutes or until just set in the centre. Leave to cool in the tin and then cut into squares.

FLORENTINES

Sweet and rich these are great with after-dinner coffee and liqueurs.

MAKES: 12
BAKING TIME: 7–10 MINUTES

INGREDIENTS
50g unsalted butter
50g caster sugar
2 tablespoons double cream
2 tablespoons chopped angelica
3 tablespoons chopped mixed peel
3 tablespoons sultanas
5 glacé cherries, chopped
40g flaked almonds, lightly crushed
1 tablespoon plain flour
125g plain or white chocolate, chopped

1. Preheat the oven to 180°C/350°F/Gas mark 4. Put the butter and sugar into a small pan and heat gently until dissolved then bring to the boil.
2. Remove from the heat and stir in all the ingredients except the chocolate. Mix well together.
3. Place heaped teaspoonfuls on lightly greased or non-stick baking sheets. Space well apart to allow for spreading. Bake a few at time for about 6–8 minutes until the edges are just beginning to turn brown. Using a large plain metal biscuit cutter push the edges of each Florentine in to create a neat round. Bake for 1–2 minutes more until golden brown.
4. Cool on the baking sheet for a few minutes then transfer to a wire rack to harden.
5. Melt the chocolate in a heatproof bowl over a saucepan of simmering water. Roll the edges of each cookie in the chocolate and place on a sheet of baking paper until set.

COOKIE TIP
Rolling half the cookies in plain chocolate and the other half in white makes them into a real treat.

BRAZIL NUT Biscotti

Italians traditionally dunk their biscotti – a cookie native to their country – into espresso or vin santo (sweet wine).

MAKES: 50
BAKING TIME: 50 MINUTES

INGREDIENTS
2 eggs
175g sugar
Grated rind 1 orange
2 tablespoons orange juice
60ml light vegetable oil
200g Brazil nuts
350g plain flour
2 teaspoons baking powder
175g ground rice

1. Preheat the oven to 180°C/350°F/Gas mark 4.

2. Place the eggs and sugar in a large mixing bowl and beat until very pale and thick. Beat in the orange rind, juice and oil. Stir in the nuts.

3. Sift the flour and baking powder together and add to the bowl with the rice, working the mixture with your hands to form a soft dough. Add a little extra flour if the dough is too sticky. Divide in half and roll each piece to form a 20cm log.

4. Place the logs on the baking sheets and bake until risen and golden, about 30 minutes. Remove from the oven and cool slightly. Reduce the oven temperature to 150°C/300°F/Gas mark 2.

5. Using a serrated knife, cut the logs into thin slices and arrange on the baking sheets. Bake the slices, turning once, until crisp and golden on both sides, about 20 minutes. Store in an airtight container for several weeks.

MAPLE SYRUP Tuiles

These little treats are a great accompaniment to creamy desserts. They do require a little care when cooking. Only cook two or three at a time, as they need to be shaped fairly quickly while still very warm.

MAKES: 20
BAKING TIME: 5–7 MINUTES

INGREDIENTS
55g unsalted butter
65g soft light brown sugar
1 tablespoon maple syrup
1 tablespoon brandy
50g plain flour

COOKIE TIP
These tuiles can soften if left out, so store in an airtight container.

1. Preheat the oven to 180°C/350°F/Gas mark 4. Put the butter, sugar and syrup into a saucepan and heat gently while stirring until the sugar has dissolved. Simmer, uncovered and without stirring, for 2 minutes.
2. Remove from the heat and stir in the brandy and flour. Put 2 or 3 level teaspoonfuls on to lightly greased baking sheets. Bake in the oven for 5–7 minutes until lightly browned.
3. Remove from the oven and cool for just 1 minute and then carefully lift off the baking sheet with a spatula. Drape over a wooden rolling pin or wooden spoon handle and leave to harden. Alternatively, pinch the centre together to give a flower shape or drape over upturned egg cups to make little baskets.

CRACKLE Cookies

These look stunning and are so easy to make. As a variation try adding some chopped dark glacé cherries to the mixture.

MAKES: 24
BAKING TIME: 10 MINUTES

INGREDIENTS
60g self-raising flour
25g cocoa powder
90g caster sugar
30g butter
1 egg, beaten
1 teaspoon cherry brandy
60g icing sugar

1. Preheat the oven to 200°C/400°F/Gas mark 6. Sift the flour and cocoa into a bowl and stir in the sugar.
2. Blend in the butter until the mixture resembles fine crumbs. Stir in the egg and cherry brandy and mix well together.
3. Put the icing sugar into a bowl. Shape walnut-sized pieces of dough into balls and drop into the icing sugar. Toss until thickly coated and place on baking sheets lined with baking paper.
4. Bake for about 10 minutes until just set. Cool on a wire rack.

COOKIE TIP
If you wish you can make the dough ahead of time and keep covered in the refrigerator. Shape and bake the cookies at the last minute and serve warm.

POPPYSEED & HONEY Pinwheels

You can change the nuts and flavourings in these cookies. Try using chopped toasted almonds or macadamias, and for flavour try lemon instead of orange rind or a large pinch of ground cinnamon or ginger.

MAKES: 30
BAKING TIME: 8–10 MINUTES

INGREDIENTS
115g butter
½ teaspoon vanilla extract
115g caster sugar
1 egg
250g plain flour

FILLING
50g very finely chopped toasted hazelnuts
80g poppy seeds
60ml honey, warmed
1 teaspoon finely grated orange rind

1. Put the butter, vanilla, sugar and egg into a bowl and beat well together. Stir in the flour and shape into a ball. Wrap in clingfilm and chill until firm.

2. Put all the filling ingredients into a bowl and mix well together. Cut the dough in half and roll out each portion between sheets of baking paper, to a rectangle 20 x 25cm. Spread the filling over the two pieces of dough and roll up from the short side like a Swiss roll. Wrap in clingfilm and chill until firm.

3. Preheat the oven to 190°C/375°F/Gas mark 5. Cut the rolls into 3mm slices and place on non-stick baking sheets. Bake for about 8–10 minutes until lightly browned.

COOKIE TIP
The pastry dough is very soft to handle so make sure it is well chilled before rolling out between sheets of baking paper.

COOKIES PLUS

CAPPUCCINO Bars

The sheer variety of textures in these bars makes for a decadent treat.

MAKES: 12

INGREDIENTS
50g sultanas
125ml hot strong black coffee
300g digestive biscuits
25g mini marshmallows
225g plain chocolate
4 tablespoons butter

TOPPING
225g white chocolate
4 tablespoons butter
100g icing sugar
Grated plain chocolate

1. Lightly grease a 20 x 20cm square tin and line the base with non-stick baking paper.
2. Soak the sultanas in the hot coffee for 5 minutes. Break the digestive biscuits into small pieces and place in a bowl with the marshmallows. Sprinkle in the coffee and soaked sultanas.
3. Melt the chocolate and butter in a microwave or in a bowl set over hot water. Add to the biscuit mixture and stir until well coated. Press the mixture into the prepared cake tin and chill until firm.
4. To make the topping, melt the white chocolate in a microwave or in a bowl set over a pan of hot water. Leave to cool. Cream the butter until soft, gradually beat in the icing sugar. Beat in the melted white chocolate. Spread the mixture over the biscuit base and leave to set.
5. Sprinkle with grated chocolate and cut into bars. Store in an airtight container in a cool place for up to four days.

APPLE & RASPBERRY Bars

Apples and raspberries are a wonderfully irresistible combination.

MAKES: 12–14
BAKING TIME: 45 MINUTES

INGREDIENTS
75g unsalted butter
175g caster sugar
3 eggs
1 teaspoon vanilla extract
175g self-raising flour
4 medium cooking apples (about 450g), grated
200g raspberries

1. Preheat the oven to 190°C/375°F/Gas mark 5. Grease a 38 x 25 x 2.5cm baking tin and set aside.
2. In a large mixing bowl beat the butter with the sugar until it resembles fine breadcrumbs. Beat in the eggs and vanilla extract until combined.
3. Beat or stir in the flour, and then add the grated apple. Mix thoroughly until well combined.
4. Pour the mixture into the prepared baking tin, spreading the mixture evenly. Push the raspberries into the mixture evenly spaced around the tin. Bake for about 25 minutes or until a tester inserted in the centre comes out clean.
5. Cool in the tin and serve cut into bars or squares. Store in the refrigerator for up to four days.

CHOCOLATE & MACADAMIA NUT Bars

These bars will set as they cool, but still be wonderfully chewy.

MAKES: 9
BAKING TIME: 30–35 MINUTES

INGREDIENTS
225g butter
225g plain chocolate, cut up
120g macadamia nuts
285g soft light brown sugar
3 eggs
225g plain flour
2 teaspoons baking powder
½ teaspoon salt

1. Preheat the oven to 180°C/350°F/Gas mark 4. Melt the butter and chocolate together in a glass bowl over a saucepan of simmering water until smooth and glossy. Allow to cool slightly. Toast the macadamia nuts on a baking sheet in the oven for 5 minutes until just golden, then roughly chop.
2. Beat the sugar and eggs together in a large bowl. Carefully stir in the chocolate mixture. Fold in the flour, baking powder and salt, then stir in the chopped nuts.
3. Line the base of a 20cm square, non-stick cake tin that is at least 5cm deep. Pour in the mixture and bake for 30–35 minutes. Allow to cool in the tin.
4. Serve cut into squares with ice cream or cream.

MOCHA MUD Pies

A cookie that's rich and dense in texture like a brownie with a chocolate/coffee flavour has to be divine, and it is. Make sure the mixture is well chilled before baking.

MAKES: 16
BAKING TIME: 10 MINUTES

INGREDIENTS
30g plain flour
¼ teaspoon bicarbonate of soda
200g plain chocolate, roughly chopped
25g unsalted butter
2–3 tablespoons instant coffee granules, according to personal taste
2 large eggs
115g caster sugar
1 teaspoon vanilla extract
50g plain chocolate chips

1. Sift together the flour and bicarbonate of soda. Put the chocolate and the butter into a heatproof bowl over a saucepan of simmering water or melt in the microwave. When melted remove from the heat and stir in the coffee granules.
2. Put the eggs and sugar into a bowl and beat with an electric beater until pale and very thick. Stir in the chocolate mixture and the vanilla. Add the flour mixture and stir. Mix in the chocolate chips.
3. Cover the bowl and place in the refrigerator for about 1 hour.
4. Preheat the oven to 180°C/350°F/Gas mark 4. Line baking sheets with baking paper. Place spoonfuls of the mixture well apart on the prepared sheets.
5. Bake for about 10 minutes or until the cookies feel just set when touched lightly with a finger. Cool for a few minutes before transferring to a wire rack.

BLONDIES

These are like brownies but are made with white chocolate and sugar instead of brown – even more irresistible.

MAKES: 18
BAKING TIME: 30–35 MINUTES

INGREDIENTS
500g white chocolate
75g butter
3 eggs
180g caster sugar
180g self-raising flour
180g macadamia nuts, roughly chopped
1 teaspoon vanilla extract

1. Preheat the oven to 190°C/375°F/Gas mark 5. Grease and base line a 26 x 19cm baking pan.
2. Roughly chop 400g of the chocolate and put aside.
3. Melt the remaining chocolate and the butter in a bowl over a saucepan of simmering water. Cool slightly.
4. Beat the eggs and sugar together in a bowl and gradually beat in the melted chocolate. Sift the flour over the mixture and fold in together with the chopped nuts, reserved chocolate and vanilla extract.
5. Pour into the prepared tin and bake for 30–35 minutes until the centre is only just firm to the touch. Cool in the tin. Cut into squares when cold.

COOKIE TIP

Store bar cookies either in tightly covered containers or in the tin in which they were baked. Make sure you cover the tin tightly with aluminium foil.

MUESLI, HONEY & DATE Health Bars

Although muesli is packed full of goodness, it can be very high in calories. Read the labels of packet muesli when buying to make sure that these bars have all the health benefits of muesli without the fat!

MAKES: 10
BAKING TIME: 20–25 MINUTES

INGREDIENTS
150g butter
6 tablespoons soft light brown sugar, firmly packed
75g honey
175g muesli
75g rolled oats
100g dates, chopped

1. Preheat the oven to 190°C/375°F/Gas mark. Grease a 20 x 20cm square cake pan and line the bottom with non-stick baking paper.
2. Melt the butter with the sugar and honey in a saucepan, stirring thoroughly until well combined.
3. Remove from the heat and stir in the muesli, oats, and dates. Turn into the cake tin and press down lightly. Bake until firm, 20–25 minutes.
4. Cool for a few minutes in the tin, then cut into bars and let cool completely. Store in an airtight container for up to two weeks.

COOKIE TIP
For even cooking bake the bars on the middle shelf of your oven.

HAZELNUT & CHOCOLATE Bars

Toasting the hazelnuts in this recipe really brings out the nutty flavour.

MAKES: 12
BAKING TIME: 25 MINUTES

INGREDIENTS
75g plain chocolate
125g butter, softened
50g soft light brown sugar
100g plain flour
75g rolled oats
12 tablespoons chocolate hazelnut spread, such as Nutella
50g hazelnuts, chopped and toasted

1. Preheat the oven to 180°C/350°F/Gas mark 4. Lightly grease a 20 x 20cm square cake tin and line the base with non-stick baking paper.

2. Melt the chocolate in a microwave or in a bowl set over a saucepan of simmering water. Cream the butter and sugar together until light and fluffy. Beat in the chocolate, then mix in the flour and oats to form a soft dough.

3. Press the mixture into the base of the prepared tin and bake until just golden, about 25 minutes.

4. Cool in the tin. Remove from the tin and spread with chocolate hazelnut spread. Sprinkle with the hazelnuts and press lightly into the spread. Cut into bars. Store in a cool place, in a single layer in an airtight container, for up to one week.

COOKIE TIP

Keep the dough in the freezer for those chocolate cookie urges. Just remember to thaw the dough in the refrigerator for several hours for easier slicing.

NUTTY BUBBLE Bars

A treat for all those peanut lovers and a great way to use up leftover cereal.

MAKES: 24

INGREDIENTS
125g butter
80ml golden syrup
80g smooth peanut butter
100g caster sugar
70g rice bubble cereal
90g coco bubble cereal
50g peanut brittle, chopped
50g chopped toasted hazelnuts

1. Base line a 24 x 30cm baking tin with baking paper.
2. Mix together the butter, golden syrup, peanut butter and sugar in a medium saucepan. Heat gently while stirring, until the sugar dissolves. Bring to the boil and simmer very gently, uncovered, without stirring for 5 minutes.
3. Remove from the heat and stir in all the remaining ingredients. Spread into the prepared tin and chill. When set cut into bars.

COOKIE TIP

To prevent the golden syrup from clinging to the side of the measuring cup, lightly grease the cup first or spray it with nonstick cooking spray.

TANGY CREAM CHEESE Bars

Cream cheese blends best if allowed to soften at room temperature for a good hour before mixing.

MAKES: 18
BAKING TIME: 25–30 MINUTES

INGREDIENTS
175g butter, softened
100g full-fat cream cheese
175g sugar
1 egg
2 tablespoons orange juice
2 tablespoons lemon juice
75g mixed peel
350g plain flour
1 teaspoon baking powder

ICING
100g icing sugar
1 tablespoon orange or lemon juice

1. Preheat the oven to 190°C/375°F/Gas mark 5. Grease a shallow 23 x 23cm square tin.

2. Beat the butter and cream cheese together, then add the sugar and continue to beat until pale and fluffy. Beat in the egg. Beat in the fruit juices and stir in the mixed candied peel.

3. Sift the flour and baking powder together and add to the mixture to form a soft dough. Roll out on a lightly floured surface to a square that will fit the base of the prepared tin. Place in tin.

4. Bake until golden, 25–30 minutes. Cool in the tin.

5. Cut into bars. Sift the icing sugar into a small bowl and stir in enough juice to make a smooth icing. Drizzle the icing over the bars and let set.

COOKIE TIP

Be sure to store these in the refrigerator as cream cheese is perishable.

GINGER OAT Squares

A crisp base and a chewy ginger oat topping give these cookies a fabulous contrast of textures.

MAKES: 12
BAKING TIME: 25 MINUTES

INGREDIENTS
175g plain flour
1 teaspoon ground ginger
125g butter
50g soft light brown sugar
1–2 tablespoons water
TOPPING
4 pieces stem ginger in syrup
3 tablespoons stem ginger syrup
4 tablespoons butter
2 tablespoons soft light brown sugar
100g rolled oats

1. Preheat the oven to 190°C/375°F/Gas mark 5. Lightly grease a 23 x 23cm square tin.

2. Place the flour and ground ginger in a mixing bowl and rub in the butter until the mixture resembles fine breadcrumbs. Stir in the sugar. Add enough water to mix to a soft dough. Roll out and use to line the base of the tin.

3. To make the topping: chop the ginger. Place in a saucepan with the syrup, butter, and sugar. Heat gently, stirring until the butter melts and the mixture is well blended.

4. Stir in the oats. Spread the mixture evenly over the dough. Bake until golden brown, about 25 minutes. Cool in the tin and cut into squares to serve.

APRICOT & ALMOND Slices

For a chewy, nutty flavour that is out of this world, you can't beat these fruit slices.

MAKES: 16
BAKING TIME: 20 MINUTES

INGREDIENTS
300g plain flour
3 tablespoons icing sugar
1 teaspoon baking powder
175g butter
2 egg yolks

TOPPING
60g apricot jam
2 egg whites
100g sugar
50g ground almonds
50g sliced almonds

GLAZE
60g apricot jam

1. Preheat the oven to 190°C/375°F/Gas mark 5. Lightly grease a 23 x 23cm square baking tin.

2. Sift the flour, icing sugar, and baking powder into a mixing bowl. Cut the butter into cubes and blend until the mixture resembles fine breadcrumbs. Stir in the egg yolks. Using your fingertips, work the mixture together to form a smooth dough, adding a little cold water if necessary. Roll or press out the dough to fit the base of the prepared tin and prick all over with a fork. Bake until just golden, about 10 minutes. Remove from the oven.

3. To make the topping: spread the apricot jam over the crust. Beat the egg whites until frothy but not stiff. Stir in the sugar and ground almonds. Spread over the jam and sprinkle the sliced almonds on top. Return to the oven until golden brown, about 20 minutes. Cool in the tin. Carefully remove the pastry from the tin.

4. To make the glaze: melt the apricot jam with 1 tablespoon water and brush over the surface to glaze. Cut into triangles to serve.

FIG & CINNAMON Slices

Delicious on their own these fig slices also make a great dessert served with vanilla ice cream.

MAKES: 24–30
BAKING TIME: 10 MINUTES

INGREDIENTS
125g butter
50g soft light brown sugar
1 teaspoon ground cinnamon
180g plain flour
375g dried figs
1 cinnamon stick
125g caster sugar
Finely grated rind of 1 lemon

1. Preheat the oven to 180°C/350°F/Gas mark 4. Lightly grease and base line a 26 x 18cm baking tin.

2. Beat together the butter, brown sugar and cinnamon until creamy. Mix in the flour and then press the mixture evenly into the tin pressing down with the back of a spoon or your fingertips. Bake for 15 minutes until golden but not brown.

3. Meanwhile put the figs, cinnamon stick, sugar and 375ml boiling water into a saucepan. Bring to the boil, stirring. Reduce the heat and simmer gently for 15 minutes until the figs have softened and water reduced by about a third.

4. Remove the cinnamon stick. Add the lemon rind. Process the mixture until smooth in a food processor.

5. Spread the fig purée over the cooked base and bake for 10 minutes until set. Cool in the tin. Cut into squares when cold.

COOKIE TIP

Only store one kind of cookie in a container. If you mix crisp and soft cookies they will all go soft and end up tasting the same.

HAZELNUT & CINNAMON Meringues

A soft slightly chewy meringue with a warm spicy flavour.

MAKES: 50
BAKING TIME: 45 MINUTES

INGREDIENTS
3 egg whites
150g caster sugar
85g ground hazelnuts
1 teaspoon ground cinnamon
250g milk chocolate

COOKIE TIP
Alternatively, you can use ground almonds and use plain chocolate instead of milk chocolate.

1. Preheat the oven to 120°C/250°F/Gas mark 1. Line baking sheets with baking paper.
2. Put the egg whites into a bowl and beat with a hand-held electric beater until the mixture stands in soft peaks. Beat in the sugar a little at a time, beating well between each addition. Fold in the nuts and cinnamon.
3. Put the mixture into a piping bag fitted with a large plain nozzle. Pipe in 5cm rounds on the prepared baking sheets. Flatten the tops with a wetted spatula.
4. Bake in the oven for about 45 minutes until dry to the touch. Turn the oven off leaving the meringues in the oven to dry out.
5. Melt the chocolate in the microwave or in a bowl over a saucepan of hot water. Either half dip the meringues in the chocolate or just coat the edges. Leave to set on baking paper.

CITRUS Squares

These fruity squares pack a real citrus punch to perk up your afternoon.

MAKES: 15
BAKING TIME: 32–40 MINUTES

INGREDIENTS
125g plain flour
40g icing sugar
100g unsalted butter

TOPPING
2 eggs
170g golden caster sugar
Finely grated rind of lemon
Finely grated rind of 1 small orange
4 tablespoons lime juice
1 tablespoon plain flour
½ teaspoon bicarbonate soda

1. Preheat the oven to 180°C/350°F/Gas mark 4. Grease and base line a 26 x 19cm shallow baking tin.

2. Put the flour, icing sugar, and butter into a food processor. Using the pulse button, process until the mixture comes together to make a firm dough. Press the dough evenly into the prepared tin and bake for 12–15 minutes until golden but not brown.

3. Beat the eggs until frothy. Gradually beat in the sugar and continue until the mixture is thick and foamy. Beat in the lemon and orange rind and lime juice. Beat in the flour and bicarbonate of soda. Pour over the baked base. Bake for 20–25 minutes until golden brown.

4. Cool in the tin and then cut into squares.

COOKIE TIP
If a recipe calls for both lemon rind and juice, pour the lemon juice over the rind to keep it moist.

NO-BAKE CHOCOLATE FUDGE Bars

The beauty of these bars is their simplicity—and their unadulterated chocolate hit!

MAKES: 12

INGREDIENTS
225g vanilla wafers
125g butter
2 tablespoons golden syrup
2 tablespoons cocoa powder
100g milk chocolate, broken into pieces
3 tablespoons icing sugar
2 tablespoons milk

1. Lightly grease an 20 x 20cm square tin. Place the wafers in a plastic bag and crush to produce fine crumbs with a rolling pin. Alternatively, process the wafers to crumbs in a food processor.
2. Place the butter, golden syrup, and cocoa in a small saucepan and heat gently until melted and blended, while stirring. Add the crumbs and stir until well combined.
3. Press the mixture into the tin and chill until firm, at least 1 hour.
4. Melt the chocolate together with the icing sugar and milk in a small bowl over a saucepan of hot water. Spread over the crumb crust and set before cutting into bars.

COOKIE TIP

Most icing sugar is blended with a small amount of cornflour to prevent major lumping. Even so, it's usually best to sift it prior to use.

PEPPERMINT CHOC Sticks

These biscuits are deceptively easy to make and are absolutely delicious served with coffee at the end of a meal.

MAKES: 12–15

INGREDIENTS
250g plain chocolate
50g clear hard peppermints, crushed
150g Amaretti biscuits, crushed

1. Melt the chocolate in a heatproof bowl over a saucepan of simmering water.
2. Remove from the heat and allow to cool slightly. Stir in the remaining ingredients.
3. Place a 30 x 10cm sheet of baking paper on a baking sheet. Spread the mixture evenly over the paper leaving a narrow edge. Allow to set.
4. When firm use a saw edge knife and carefully cut into thin sticks.

COOKIE TIP

Because this is such an easy recipe to make, it gives you more time to be creative with the shape of the cookie. Instead of sticks the mixture can be spread out and cut into thin squares or disks.

INDEX

O

P

RECIPE CREDITS

JACQUELINE BELLEFONTAINE

Pages 20, 21, 24, 25, 26 ,27, 28, 29, 32, 34, 35, 39, 44, 45, 48, 49, 50, 51, 54, 55, 56, 57, 58, 59, 62, 70, 71, 74, 75, 78, 69, 82, 83, 84, 86, 88, 94, 99, 120, 122, 123, 124, 125, 126, 128, 129, 130, 131, 132, 139, 144, 145, 146, 147, 150, 151, 154, 155, 159, 166, 168, 172, 173, 176, 177, 178, 183

VALERIE BARRETT

Pages 22, 30, 33, 36, 38, 40, 52, 60, 63, 66, 72, 76, 80, 89, 90, 96, 100, 101, 102, 104, 106, 107, 108, 110, 112, 114, 115, 116, 134, 136, 137, 138, 152, 156, 158, 160, 162, 163, 169, 170, 174, 179, 180, 182, 184

LORNA BRASH

Pages 95, 98, 105, 111

JENNY WHITE

Pages 87, 140, 148

MAGGIE MAYHEW

Pages 64, 65, 133

PHOTOGRAPHY CREDITS

MARIE LOUISE AVERY

Pages 2, 7 top, 8, 9, 10, 11, 13, 14, 16 left, 17, 18–19, 22, 31, 36, 42–43, 47, 52, 61, 63, 66, 68–69, 73, 77, 81, 85, 91, 92–93, 97, 103, 109, 113, 117, 118–119, 121, 127, 135, 141, 142–143, 149, 152, 157, 161, 164–165, 171, 175, 181, 185

CHRIS ALACK

Pages 3, 5, 6, 7 bottom, 15, 16 right, 20, 24, 29, 32, 34, 35, 39, 49, 50, 55, 56, 58, 59, 62, 64, 70, 78, 86, 88, 94, 95, 98, 105, 111, 122, 125, 129, 130, 132, 139, 145, 147, 151, 154, 155, 159, 167, 169, 172, 173, 177, 178